OUR BATTLE WITH SATAN'S SIDEKICK

THE HAUNTINGS OF TWO SISTERS

Pam Mandel with Karen Pena

Printed in the United States of America

ISBN: 978-1-7351047-2-0 (paperback)
ISBN: 978-1-7351047-3-7 (ebook)

Canoe Tree
Press

4697 Main Street
Manchester Center, VT 05255

Canoe Tree Press is a division of DartFrog Books.

*We dedicate this book to our Dead Mother who taught us
that death is just another part of the adventure.*

FOREWORD

What do you do when real evil straight out of the gates of Hell enters your life? But not just enters your life, actually moves into your home. Karen and Pam's stories take you on the most unbelievable journey surrounding a horrific battle between good and evil. A fight between God and Satan. And finally, multiple confrontations between a Christian and a Satan worshiper. Martin Luther King once said, "To ignore evil is to become an accomplice to it." So, we fought it with a maniacal energy. It's a reality-based 24/7 roller-coaster ride of what a Satan worshiper is capable of!

A few months ago, Sidekick (the Satan worshiper who was also Karen's daughter's boyfriend) was having a whopper of a meltdown in her presence. She responded by telling him that he needed to get down on his knees and give his heart to God. Obviously, when he moved in with them, no one, including her daughter, knew what he was up to in the middle of the night. *(Psalms 104:20 "Thou makest darkness, and it is night: wherein all the beasts of the forest do creep forth.")* He responded to Karen's suggestion by looking straight in her eyes and laughing, insisting that Heaven was a joke and that he was proudly on his way to Hell! In addition, he added he would very likely be a soldier of high rank, since he'd spent most of his life working towards that honor.

His words frightened her. I mean really, who on earth talks like that? At that moment she thought that she had just been treated to an omniscient look at his vicious agenda. Suddenly she realized that if he could destroy and kill a strong Christian like her, it would serve as a big boost to his plan to work his way up the ladder of Hell's Army.

Karen and Pam address this in their book, presenting a very dark perspective indeed on what it is like to live with a serious Satan worshiper as well as the consequences that follow from this experience.

They made the terrifying decision to write this book while Karen was still living in Hell's sublet. They knew that their lives were in jeopardy by writing these stories. Nonetheless, they felt very passionate about people needing to be aware that demons are not just shadows in the dark. They are not just noise makers or ghosts playing at spiritual games. It is deadly serious, and they ALWAYS have an agenda! It could be as diabolical as destroying a loving relationship, or as evil as influencing you to take your own life or someone else's.

It is absolutely crazy and hard to believe that they have actually survived and lived through this nightmare! Number one on their "Top Ten List" is what they call "The Demonic Fog." You will see this term used over and over in the book because it is the demon's most useful and most devastating trick. By compelling you to think that you are in a completely different reality, they are able to direct and redirect the human mind. If ever you reach this point in your dealings with them, you are in grave danger!

Their fervor in writing this book is to expose the Satan worshiper's dark nature and their dirty little secrets and to expose their book of tricks that they have deployed for eons to harm and destroy others' lives.

Be aware that the Satan worshiper's goal is to deceive and blend in to society. Most of the time they are not going to be wearing your stereotypical black attire. They can be celebrities, music stars, politicians, the wealthy elite or your average neighbor or co-worker. They can be charming and charismatic. Christians need to ask God to reveal who they are and to protect them from the harm they can cause. *(Psalm 28:3 "Do not drag me away with the wicked, with those who do evil, who speak cordially with their neighbors but harbor malice in their hearts.")*

This is not another book on demons. This is a first-hand, in-your-face account of what it is like to co-exist with Lucifer's demons on a daily basis, 24/7. Karen and Pam have never claimed to be paranormal experts. The gifts they've been given and their experiences, nonetheless, could not be more real. They are living proof that Satan worshipers exist on earth, so be forewarned!

This may well be one of the scariest books you have ever read.

DEMONS' TOP TEN LIST

1. Demonic Fog
2. Physically and Mentally Intimidate
3. Revenge/Retaliation
4. Disastrous Agendas for Victims
5. Device/Electronics Manipulators (even Medical Devices)
6. Transforms into Different Images
7. Send Their Pets to Terrorize You
8. Play Mind Games
9. Energy Drainers
10. They Watch Your Every Move

DEMON BLOCK

I sat down at my computer early this morning with a freshly made cup of coffee, all psyched up about starting on this book's first chapter. No sooner had I typed "Chapter One" on my Mac than my full cup of coffee went flying across my desk, in front of me, with its contents spilling all over the desk top. As the dark liquid spilled over the sides and onto the floor, an extremely dark and creepy male voice whispered in my ear, "Was that hilarious?"

But first, some background. Earlier that morning, during a discussion over the phone that I was having with my sister, we were discussing our recent experiences with demons and how humor was a useful coping mechanism for dealing with that entire realm. One point on which we were in full agreement had to do with how often demons can be hilariously petty.

That's one of the first things I learned about demons is that they hear everything! You see, shortly after I let the minions (our term for demons) know that the flying coffee cup would be covered at the beginning of Chapter One, my sister called to inform me that her desk started to shake violently as soon as she started to email me my notes for the book! Since she lives in the San Francisco Bay Area in California, earthquake country, she took a second look around to see if anything else was behaving similarly in her house. Seeing that the only thing moving, rocking or swaying was her desk, she got back on her computer and pressed the send button.

I am dying and I know it.

Sad to say, but at this moment I am the only one in the house that is aware of this fact. You see, both my husband and daughter have been held incommunicado, I believe, in a sort of supernatural fog by the demons that have been haunting me mercilessly for the last several months. I call it the "Demonic Fog," (#1 on our Top Ten List) and I have only become aware of this entity recently.

In essence, I am in a battlefield; at this point I am afraid that my armies are on the losing end of every encounter. My face is ravaged by deep sores and my legs are so thin that my bones, from ankle to high hip, are clearly visible. In the past 60 days I have lost close to 30 pounds, and as the vomiting and diarrhea continue without relief on an hourly basis, the weight loss continues unabated. Too weak to leave my bed, let alone make it to the ER on my own, my repeated attempts to make it clear to my husband that I was extremely ill were foiled by the Demonic Fog that had all but imprisoned him. The result is that my tearful pleading is being met with dead eyes and an utter lack of comprehension.

I fear that my already severe diabetes will be made even worse by the inability to keep any of my medications down, an outcome made even more likely by the vomiting and diarrhea-induced stress that have invaded my body. My sugars are completely out of control and I am now in a state of ketoacidosis. My breathing is quickly becoming shallow. All this adds up to the last straw for my sister, Pam, who lives in California. She calls an ambulance and then my husband.

But I regress. Let's start at the beginning. . . .

My husband, daughter and I had a six-year plan. She lived with us for four years, saving everything she could, then bought her first beautiful new home. The plan was that we would live with her for a few years so we could finally recover from the 2008 economic crash.

Sounds like a simple plan, right? Unfortunately, it became very complicated.

In August of 2018, my dead mother warned my sister Pam: "Karen and her hubby should not move in with Jennifer. Her boyfriend has a dark side!" Of course, Pam immediately called to pass the news on to me. After a long discussion, we concluded that "dark side" might have been a reference to a bad temper or a sour disposition. Looking back on it, I can see how clueless we both were! The thing is, my dead mother was relentless in her campaign to keep me from making a horrible mistake, hence the warning she gave again and again to my sister: "Jennifer's boyfriend has a dark side!" My sister eventually became adamant about us not moving in with my daughter, even though it had all been decided a while back. She was so insistent that she told me that if we go to marriage counseling for 10 sessions to discuss it, she would be happy to pay for it.

We went to counseling.

Then I gave in to my husband and went back to our original six-year plan.

Now that I have 20/20 vision that comes with hindsight, I can share the priceless lesson I learned from all of this. When a dear departed loved one gives you an important message from the afterlife, it is more subtle and vague than in our dimension. But despite the extra work it may take to decipher it, it's well worth the effort. What can I say, maybe it's just one of those rules that are in effect in the afterlife? Bottom line: Listen to your dead mother! I wish I had.

We moved into the house on February 22, 2019, about two months after my daughter had moved in. Her boyfriend (whom we will refer to as Sidekick from now on) had been staying with her off and on for some time before we had moved in. At the time, he was still going back and forth from where he previously lived. My sister, Pam, arrived the same day, the 22nd, to help me make the transition from old house to new home.

Pam hadn't even been in the house 10 minutes when, walking downstairs from the guest room, she spotted a demon coming in from the left wall of the living room (yes, you read right) after which he walked across the family room into the kitchen and quite literally disappeared! According to Pam, this was no ordinary demon. Big, tall and well-muscled, his exaggerated swagger implied that he had as much of a right to be there as anyone else (remember, this is a brand-new house)! At first my sister was convinced that this creature simply belonged to the land, like any furry little critter or slimy, scaly snake you might inherit with the purchase of the property on which a new house sits. This was different, however, and she just couldn't stop dwelling on the image that had made itself at home in her mind earlier. The way he swaggered across the living room as well as the aura of arrogance that emanated from him alarmed her greatly and gave her serious cause for concern. Basically, he acted as if it was his home, and we were the intruders.

When she spoke to me about it, I too was puzzled. What the hell, I thought, but as a "sensitive" I opened myself up partially to feel what was going on in the house. It took me two days to figure out that the demon's attachment was not to a "what" (the land) but to a "who"–Sidekick! When I shared this insight with my sister, she was so taken aback by it that we immediately started to argue. I remember her reaction very clearly. She kept insisting that Sidekick is the nicest guy; why would he have a demon close to him? *(Matthew 7:15 "Beware of false prophets, which come to you in sheep's clothing, but inwardly they are ravening wolves.")* After a while, though, she agreed with me. For Pam and me this was very disturbing indeed, and at the time that's all we could comprehend. My sister has the ability to see and hear into the other dimension. By this point, we were both desperately seeking answers while being extra careful not to drop our guard.

Interesting sidebar . . . one day, while my sister and Sidekick were in the car, he started drilling her about these gifts of hers. He maintained a somewhat casual and light tone, thus avoiding putting Pam on her guard. Besides, Pam is open and honest by nature, and so was happy to answer his questions about this topic (again, how clueless we both were!). Unfortunately, the information she gave to Sidekick would come back to haunt her again and again.

Note to reader: We described the following week, the week my sister helped me move in, in our first book *The Hauntings of Two Sisters—Shocking True Life Experiences* in the chapter "Six Nights of Horror," but for those of you who did not read it, I will recount the highlights of her experiences that week.

First night . . . about an hour after midnight, my sister was awakened by a very creepy feeling. She reacted by checking the room. Then all of a sudden, her bed started shaking violently! As if that wasn't awful enough, just after doing so, she herself was face to face with a big dark mass looming scarily over her. Utterly terrified, she buried her head in her pillow and prayed until it finally disappeared.

Second night . . . around 1:30 am she began hearing loud obnoxious sounds coming from the loft down the hall. She managed her fear to the point where she finally got up to investigate. The fruit of her investigation was a confrontation with what was one of the most terrifying creatures she had ever seen: a huge, dark demon with large horns coming out of each side of his head, pointing outward and upward. It refused to budge; instead it just stood there, looking her right in the eye! After staring at each other for a few moments, she turned around and ran to her room, slamming the door and locking it behind her. I always laugh when people, including myself, do this—like spirits can't come through a door? Fortunately, she never saw it again that night.

Third night . . . at 3:00 am her bed started shaking violently again. She looked up. Lo and behold, there was another huge dark demon standing next to her bed and looking down at her! This demon, however, brought pets with him in the form of huge black-looking grasshoppers that crawled up the wall and onto the ceiling! She screamed, "In the name of Jesus, get out!" and when she finally opened her eyes, everything was gone.

Shall I go on?

Fourth night . . . it was early evening, and my sister was quietly sitting on the toilet in the bathroom right next to her bedroom when the dark demon with the large sideways horns walks through—yes, through!—the bathroom door. After doing so he just stood there, blocking her exit while watching her (talk about a lack of boundaries!) with a keen eye. As my sister frantically goes into full panic mode, wondering how she is ever going to leave this bathroom, he simply disappears.

An hour or so later she was lying in bed with her dog watching TV when she spots a very large black dog next to her sniffing her bedtime snacks on her nightstand! This dog actually dwarfed my sister's Goldendoodle, who weighs in at a hefty 80 lbs.! Her only thought at that precise moment was, "What the Hell?"

Thus, began our relationship with three different Hellhounds! "Send Their Pets to Terrorize You" (#7 on our Top Ten List)

Fifth night . . . more or less peaceful, unless you want to count the time when, on her way from her room to the stairwell, she heard a vicious deep growl as in, "Hello, Hellhound!"

Needless to say, by night number six she was ready to leave and never come back! Obviously, the demon she saw after being in the house only 10 minutes her first day was as surprised as she was by the fact that she could see him. "Physically and Mentally Intimidate" (#2 on our Top Ten List) This was all about intimidating my sister, not only because she can actually see them but, moreover, because she had the nerve to let me know that she had seen these visitors from the Abyss. Believe it or not, the intimidation tactics they'd employed up to that point were nothing compared to what was to come in the following months!

It was at this point that I felt very strongly that it was time to sit my sister down for a second time and discuss how important it was to deal with the fear factor. The first time was in our first book at her vacation home. I did my best to impress upon her my certainty that each and every time she showed them her fear, it emboldened them to do the same or worst to her the following night. You see, they absolutely and positively thrive on their victims' fear; it feeds their distorted sense of self as well as their colossal power trip.

My sister left my daughter's house on the sixth day with the following announcement:

"I will never be back to this house!"

2

The
Whispering
✝

Karen Pena

Two weeks after my sister left for home, I saw my first demon. I was alone in the house, downstairs in the kitchen, rummaging in the fridge for ingredients for that night's dinner. All of a sudden, a creepy, crawly something, a deeply dark, as dark as dark can be, energy started crawling up my back. I whipped my body around, already knowing all too well that what I would see would not be a pretty sight. And there it was, an enormous dark faceless shadow man standing there, staring me right in the face.

Unfortunately, this was no surprise. For the past two weeks the darkness had been gathering, like a storm, building little by little each day. As aware as I was of what was going on around me, the audacity of this "Thing", this visitor from the Abyss, in coming up behind me and subjecting my body to its revolting creepiness was too much to bear. So, I decided not to bear it. After summoning up whatever courage was in me and redirecting that stare right back at its black, featureless face, I decided to add a sound track to this heavy-duty visual riff. This track consisted of just one word:

"Really?"

No sooner was that one little ol' word out of my mouth when it vanished!

Unfortunately, this incident was not to be the only one. In the next 19 months, I would have dozens of similar encounters, and learned very quickly about "shoulder checking." Me with a quickie back massage from hell was a favorite form of intimidation for these unearthly minions. "Physically and Mentally Intimidate" (#2 on our Top Ten List).

Around the same time, something else edged its way into my awareness. I started noticing behavioral changes in my 11-year-old Pitbull, Cash. Up until then he'd been a happy-go-lucky dog. All of a sudden, he began acting strange. He got into the habit of abruptly stopping when playing, staring off into space and then cowering as if he were reacting to some invisible threat.

At other times he would suddenly, and for no apparent reason, dart underneath the nearest piece of furniture or, if I was closer, curl up behind me whimpering in fear. Since his safety has always been my main priority, this inexplicable change in his behavior got to me at the deepest level. He's my best friend and I was afraid for him . . . very afraid.

One evening, a few days later, my daughter asked me to come upstairs and take a look at something that lay just outside her bedroom door. Placed in a perfect round circle on the carpet were five items that belonged to her: a camera, a hairbrush, a wallet, a bracelet, and two barrettes. What the hell? When she actually asked me if I was responsible for this, the look with which I responded must have answered her question in no uncertain terms! I was in shock, so much so that I neglected to take a photo of these objects. Although I instinctively knew that this was some type of weird ritual, I couldn't for the life of me begin to figure out what its purpose could possibly be and who had performed it. I was looking over my shoulder for the next unpleasant surprise at this point. This heightened state of alert prompted me to do something I should never have done; I used my psychic gifts to open myself up completely, without reserve, to whatever was going on inside the house. Clueless!

Sidebar: Interestingly enough, I was not allowed in my daughter's master bedroom per Sidekick's orders. The door was kept locked at all times with no extra key. Talk about a red flag alert!

Some time had gone by. The situation had worsened by a few notches (at least), and at this point, things were beginning to get even darker. During the following weeks, my daughter spoke to me about someone or something whispering in her ear on multiple occasions. She could not make out what this deep, throaty male voice was saying. The messages' lack of clarity was typical of this type of haunting and something that my sister and I had encountered on numerous occasions. Truth be told, the exact same thing had happened to my sister the first week of her stay with us, with the same ghostly entity whispering in her ear as she was making her way down the stairs. One afternoon my daughter and I were in the kitchen, comparing notes on those incidents over a cup of coffee when Sidekick just happened to walk in on our conversation to announce that he too had heard the whispering.

I have already stated that I believed that the demons were there for Sidekick. He had a very traumatic and abusive childhood, and more importantly, he had little use for and even a strong dislike for God, whom he blamed for many of the unfortunate events and circumstances of his life. Consequently, I was convinced at this point that the demons had attached themselves to him at a very early age. In the final analysis, I saw Sidekick as a victim who was being influenced and harassed by the bad guys. As a born-again Christian since the age of twelve, the only thing I felt I could do was my best to help save him.

I was utterly clueless as to how I would handle the discussion between Sidekick and myself, a discussion that I was positive had to take place without any further delay. So, in this case, I was up the proverbial creek without the proverbial paddle and getting more and more unsure of which course of action to take. And here's the clincher, maybe even the key to this whole story: I did the dumbest thing I could ever do. I told him what I was thinking, something I would have thought better about doing had I not denied what the look on his face was plainly telling me. I saw intense anger that I had approached him with God.

The issue was that I had known Sidekick since he was a teenager and had all the empathy in the world for him. After all, he and Jennifer were of the same age, and his family lived close to us. Not surprisingly, the two of them quickly became good buddies and, eventually, best friends. When we moved away, Sidekick came and stayed with us on many occasions. (I will address this in Chapter 10 "Our Light Bulb Moment.") While this familiarity encouraged me to share my deepest thoughts concerning the demons surrounding him, it also, unfortunately, empowered him in precisely the wrong way.

Why am I telling you all of this? Why, you may ask, is it so important? It's important because of my absolute faith in God. You see, I was sure that God would save him, that the demons would go away and that everything would be okay. I remember growing up in church and the altar calls that took place every Sunday. People who wanted to accept Jesus as their savior would take that long walk up to the front of the church and get on their knees and accept God. Sidekick, however, wasn't asking to accept God;

rather it was someone else, namely myself, asking him to do so. I actually told him he needed to get down on his knees before God and give his heart to Jesus. How arrogant, naïve and clueless of me! Call it whatever you like, I was an idiot with a good heart.

I began by asking him if he had ever seen anything unusual throughout his life. He answered in the affirmative, explaining that he had seen shadow figures at his grandmother's house whenever he had stayed with her. He seemed to be terrified and confused after sharing that bit of information, and oh, how my heart went out to him! At this moment, however, as I am writing all of this down, my father's words are echoing in my head: "Karen, you are such a bleeding heart."

Then something happened! My head woke up and instructed my bleeding heart to sit this one out for now. Starting that same night, I began to hear strange noises after dark. I am a hopeless insomniac and have been for decades. Our bathroom is right underneath my daughter's enormous master bedroom closet. I began to hear the nightly sound of dice or something like that being thrown over and over again, a sound that was punctuated by some weird chanting as well. Then the sound of footsteps, belonging to someone, pacing up and down for hours.

What the hell?

Very quickly, I remembered the five items arranged in a circle outside my daughter's bedroom door and I began to put two and two together.

Someone in the house was performing rituals,

something I had never encountered before.

As convincing as the evidence was, I still could not believe at that point that all of this was being done by someone I had known and cared about for years. Even more importantly, the person that my sweet, intelligent daughter loved so much!

3

Nightly
Tortures
✝

Karen Pena

There was a supernatural war going on in this house, good versus evil, God versus Satan. As of yet, I didn't know why this was happening; I just knew that as a Christian and sensitive, I was struggling daily with the moment by moment battle between these two forces. I also knew that God and Satan could not continue to co-exist in that small space. Myself representing God and good; the demons representing evil and Satan. To say it was not a situation I ever expected to find myself in would be a gross understatement. The fact of the matter is that in a million years, I would never have imagined myself in this predicament. Who would? This was supposed to be a joyous time for my husband and me. We were going to enjoy some much-needed rest and fun, but life has a way of throwing you curve balls, and this was an enormous one. The only thing that made it bearable was that as bad as things were, I knew that God was there protecting me.

At this point, there were probably a dozen demons in the house, as well as their pets (#7 on our Top Ten List). Christian or not, even under God's protection, no one can survive in that environment without repercussions. If there's one thing I know about demons, they will attack where you are most vulnerable, be it your body, mind or spirit.

No doubt about it, Satan's minions were focused on me. I was severely handicapped regarding my ability to deal with them because although my faith and mind were strong, my body was not. Not having a clue as to what or whom I was dealing with clearly gave the minions the upper hand. The first thing that started to deteriorate was my health. The pain in my body was intense. At times, I couldn't even get out of bed. I was paralyzed. I felt like the very life was being sucked right out of me so much so that I would break down and cry for no apparent reason. When I did leave my room, Sidekick would, at times, ver-bally attack me; this happened a minimum of two to three times a week. He would have these meltdowns that went on for hours, throwing things, slamming doors, yelling to himself at an ear-shattering volume. However, my husband and daughter were at work, meaning I was the only one witnessing this sporadic behavior. Finally, I started to share with my husband and daughter how Sidekick was acting. Their response was, "Stay away from him." Great advice, guys. I mean, thanks! Do tell, though, just how am I supposed to implement this brilliant plan, seeing as how he and I live under the same roof!? I honestly don't think that they really believed me. Panic mode!

As my misery grew, with no support from my loved ones, the soul-encompassing sadness that had invaded my insides grew with each passing day. As contentment was my normal state, this was not my usual take on things. Cheerfulness is the default setting in my family. Like my mother and grandmother before me, I have never been one for moodiness. This was a big emotional shift for me. I soon began to spend the entire day in bed, unable to motivate myself for anything but a visit to the bathroom. Add to that my inability to use the kitchen, the verbal abuse I suffered from my daughter's boyfriend, the soul-numbing in which I was starting to drown. Add to that the fact that no one in the house believed me, and perhaps you can get a better feel for what I was going through.

It was at that time I believe I was beginning to sound crazy to my family. That is, to everyone except my sister.

It was at this point the nightly torture started.

I have restless leg syndrome. Even though I'd been

prescribed pills to combat it, it began to spread throughout my entire body. The resulting spasms continually racked my body until they got to be so bad that I felt I was going to literally burst out of my skin. At that point my medication was useless, despite it always having worked for me in the past. I knew darn well by then that this was something different. Not being able to lay down or sleep, I would walk the house the entire night with just the demons for company— night after night, week after week, month after month. "Energy Drainers" (#9 on our Top Ten List)

One night at around 3 a.m. I was on my way to the kitchen for something to drink when I heard voices coming from the living room. Lo and behold, it was the demons having some sort of "guild meeting" in the middle of the living room. Since they were all talking at once, it was almost impossible to make out what they were saying. Nonetheless, there was one very creepy voice that was strong enough to be heard above the chatter. I could see that there was an obvious hierarchy here. It looked as though Mr. Creepy Voice was the one in charge. Two words spoken by him drowned out, in volume, frequency and intensity, all else that was said in their conversation: "plan" and "agenda." But when I came around the corner into the living room, all talking ceased. I was still able to get a glimpse of a pair of these ghouls moving away.

Of all the stories I can share, at this point, I want to share what I call the smoking demon story. At that time in my life, I was a smoker and again I am walking the house all through the night unable to sleep. Around 2:00 am I went into the backyard to have a cigarette. I was sleep deprived and honestly, an emotional mess. I sat down in my smoking chair, lit my cigarette, took a few puffs when all of a sudden, this horrific-looking demon bent right over me with his face an inch from mine! Surprisingly, this particular demon actually had a face. He had four-inch horns at the front of his head, one on each side, squinty eyes and his mouth was opened, full of pointed jagged teeth as if something had filed them sharp. No sooner had the sight of those gruesome horns and teeth taken my consciousness hostage, when a very distasteful thought came to me. Was this extremely unappealing creature actually smiling at me? Standing next to him was a four-legged representative of the Nether Regions, a hellhound whose breed I immediately recognized. He was a grey Italian Cane Corso, a truly beautiful dog despite where he came from. He was so big that his back was almost level with the demon's waist.

Then, exhausted from a lack of sleep, I was graced with a formidable courage that sometimes comes to those who are just too tired to care. Blowing a stream of smoke right in its hideous face, I then proceeded to tell him off in no uncertain terms. I believe my exact words were, "You evil piece of shit! How dare you try to intimidate me like this! You chose the wrong side and you don't even have your wings anymore! How's your undying reverence to your master Satan working out for you?!" Speech delivered, I put my cigarette out and went back in the house. Well this was not the smartest move. From then on, the house's designated ghoul pack always accompanied me when I went out into the back yard for a smoke.

Interestingly enough, every single nocturnal attack I suffered coincided with a demonic attack on my sister. Afterall, Sidekick hated her as much as me, being that she saw the demon after only being in the new house for 10 minutes. What a shock for him!

Here's a catalog of some of the attacks my sister endured in her own words.

RAIN SHOWER ATTACK

A few weeks after returning home after helping my sister move in with her daughter, I was sitting up in bed one night watching TV while making out my grocery list for the next day. My husband was already in a deep sleep when I heard the sound of water falling onto the floor just a few inches from the side of my bed. I looked around the room to see where it could be coming from. However, I didn't see any water at all, but the sound was getting louder and louder and closer and closer! I knew by the sound that the leak had to be close to where I was sitting. I quickly decided it was time to wake up Michael to let him know that something was really wrong. I reached over, tapped his arm and said, "Michael, wake up! Do you hear that? I think a water pipe broke." Before my husband could completely wake up, however, something placed its hand on my head, threw me backwards with my head hitting the headboard and held me down with a strong grip; I could neither move nor scream. The minute it touched me, the sounds of water stopped, and extreme pain started. By now, Michael was waking up. When he looked at me to see what was wrong, he was shocked to see the indentations made in my flesh by the fingers that were holding my arms down. He grabbed me and hugged me so hard, causing whatever it was that was doing this to me to stop. All he could say was, "What is happening Pam?" What exactly was happening? I had no idea. What made it even weirder was the fact that neither one of us actually saw anyone or anything grabbing me, leaving me to wonder if it was something that followed me home from my sister's house.

WHITE MIST OF EYES

One night I woke up with a very bad feeling, a feeling that something evil was entering my safe space, my bedroom. I was laying on my side, facing the edge of the bed when I noticed a white mist creeping along the floor through the bedroom doorway, slowly making its way toward my side of the bed. As it approached my bed, the white mist was getting more dense and larger in size. Once it finally reached me, it slowly rose right alongside of me to a height of about six feet. Then it started to expand horizontally to a width of approximately four feet. Now the white mist was totally solid! In a split second this huge mist started to curve down towards me. All of a sudden, thousands of eyes extended themselves from this massive thing: coal-black bumper-to-bumper eyes with the thickest imaginable eyelids. Then it shifted position so that it hovered directly over me, and that is when the pain throughout my body became almost unbearable. This circus of horrors ended on an unexpected note. Mercifully, just when I thought I couldn't take the pain anymore, it suddenly ended just as fast as it started and this "Thing" disappeared in a flash. I was so shocked! What the hell was it? Could I have been dreaming? But I knew without a doubt that I was totally awake. In fact, more awake than you could imagine!

HELLHOUND 1

One night, my husband and I were watching television in the living room when we both heard the sound of metal scratching a hard surface coming from the kitchen. It sounded like a dog's metal collar hitting the side of our kitchen sink. My husband glanced over and saw a flash of a large dog's head, dark in color, drop down, and then it was gone. Michael admitted his confusion to me. First of all, our dogs are sable in color and this one was black, very black. Secondly, our dogs were nowhere around. What was it? Could it have been the hellhound that I had seen on several occasions at my sister's house?

HELLHOUND 2

On another evening, at about 1:00 am I was awakened by something sniffing my face. It took me a few seconds to realize what was going on, thinking it was my 80-pound Goldendoodle. As I opened my eyes, I saw the butt of an enormous brindled dog. It had a butt so huge that as it walked from my bedside out my bedroom door, its sheer mass caused the butt to shift back and forth. Thinking that this monstrous hellhound had been right in my face, all I could do was thank God I didn't open my eyes until it was on its way out the door.

I immediately surveyed the room trying to locate my two dogs. I saw that our little eight-pound dog, Tucker, was right there on the bed but my Goldendoodle, Dexter, was not in sight. I ran after the hellhound to look for Dexter and was glad to see that he was sound asleep on the couch. By this time, the commotion had crested to a point where it woke my husband up. When Michael saw me come back into the bedroom, he asked me what was going on. In response to his question, I informed him that we had a hellhound in the house. Although my sister had let me know on more than one occasion that there was a new hellhound in her house (also brindle-colored), this was a first time for me.

4

The
Mighty Roar
✝

Pam Mandel

Three months had gone by since my sister had moved in with her daughter and it was hardly a walk in the park, as the saying goes. Almost 100 straight days and nights of not knowing when the next demonic attack would occur; day after day having to dig deeper and deeper into our vital reserves of energy and faith. Dealing with the spiritual oppression did seem like it was trying to steal the very oxygen from our lungs! It had all started, as you might well imagine, to take a toll on my sister's mental and physical health and her relationships as well.

I have asked myself the following question so many times: "What do you do when real evil walks into your life?" What do you do when every demonologist you've reached out to for help informs you after carefully assessing the seriousness of the situation, to lose their name and phone number and don't make contact again? Their only advice was, "Tell your sister to get the HELL out of that house now!" But the best part was, "Don't ever tell Sidekick that you talked to me or what you are planning on doing!" I was completely baffled, confused and driven to my knees in frustration. I started praying, and thankfully, an answer came immediately. I remember that once a friend of mine, Aileen, had been able to help me get free of an extremely bad spirit in our vacation home.* I decided to fill her in on our present situation, since Aileen is enlightened by the angels on a very personal level. She knows that we depend on their constant presence for protection and love, so I felt that I was being led in just the right direction in soliciting her support to invoke ALL the mighty forces from above. For as Matthew 18:20 plainly states, "For where two or three gathers in my name, there am I with them."

*Our first book, *The Hauntings of Two Sisters—Shocking True Life Experiences*, goes into details of that sorry state of affairs.

Sounds like a plan, right? After days of prayer and

spiritual preparation, it was finally time to put the plan into action. The three of us, Aileen, Karen and I were going to call on God and his Archangels to send the demons right back into Hell! Although we were all deeply aware of the difficulty of the battle ahead, we had penciled in, so to speak, a date and a time for this battle on our calendars. I think we all breathed a bit easier (I know I did) knowing that finally, the time had come to send those demons back to where they belonged.

The moment was 11:00 pm.

Aileen was in her home—praying!

Karen was in her home—praying!

I was in my home—praying!

KAREN'S STORY

Reader's Note: Please keep in mind that I was the only one who was actually in the demon house while praying. Pam and Aileen were doing it remotely. I knew God was protecting me.

It was late at night. Everyone in the house was fast asleep, and the house was so quiet that you could hear a pin drop. I was downstairs walking around and around the kitchen island in a state of deep prayer, calling on God, our spiritual protectors and the Archangel Michael. At one point, I opened my eyes and what I saw was by far the most terrifying image I had ever seen in my entire life. I knew instantly who it was: the exquisite Archangel Michael himself in full warrior attire. I instinctively jumped back without taking my eyes off him. Talk about shock and awe!

In attempting to visualize his appearance, it might help to think of an ancient Roman general in the most opulent set of armor imaginable. His protective covering was dark grey with brilliant flashes of gold throughout, and his breastplate gleamed brightly. Both biceps and forearms bulged with defined muscles, and his wrists were sheathed in wide, thick gold bracelets. His armor-plated tunic was of mid-thigh length with red pleated material peeking from underneath. A portion of his legs also bulging with muscle were bare, finishing with feet and calves encased in high black boots. He stood with his weight on his left foot, his right leg slightly bent and lifted. His mighty left arm was outstretched, pointing towards the ceiling with a long and majestic gold sword. I have never seen a more fearsome sight, and I firmly believe that I had caught him in the very act of gathering up the demons in order to throw them back into Hell.

Of all the features I'd beheld just then, I'd have to say that his face was the most terrifying of them all. Having thought long and hard on how to best describe it and having never seen anything remotely like it, the words "fierce" and "livid" come to mind. Wisps of his long, pitch-black hair reached down almost to his thick dark eyebrows. Their upward crease formed an essential element of a ferocious dark scowl, an expression made all the more terrifying by his sharply chiseled square jaw and high cheekbones. Add to all that a pair of eyes as black as a coal mine and you have the power of God Himself rendering this valiant servant of the Almighty the most frightening spectacle ever.

I would be remiss in my attempt to describe what I saw that night if I didn't mention one more thing: the golden light that surrounded him. Such was a radiance that was alive and pulsating with what I felt was the pure energy of God. No sooner had I begun to process what I had just seen than this unbelievably glorious presence was gone. It vanished in the blink of an eye. I was left standing there, overjoyed and overwhelmed by a feeling of intense gratitude for God's love, power and protection.

I returned to my bedroom for a bit, continuing my prayers. As I came out, I turned the corner into the living room and saw a dozen angels standing there lined up, side by side with their arms interlocked. I had seen this once before when my sister was having her vacation home spiritually cleansed. But this time, I believe they were there to make utterly sure that the demons did not harm me during this particular cleansing.

Pam's story: Let's take it outside!

So as not to disturb my husband from his sleep, I went into the living room, kneeled in front of the couch, and after an hour of deep prayer I was visited by a vision that I can only describe as inconceivable!

In this extraordinary vision, I was standing across the street outside of my niece's two-story house. I was viewing a large shadow demon and hellhound in her driveway and a car parked on the street, directly in front of the house. It was pitch black outside with not even a streetlight on, the only illumination being the faint bit of moonlight that provided just enough light to allow me to see what was happening.

Something drew my attention upward, where a bulky being with wings on its back was standing on the roof. At first, I was petrified! Who or what was this? Suddenly I knew without a shadow of a doubt who this had to be . . . the Archangel Michael! His statuesque physique was impressive, with swollen muscles on both his upper and lower body, his hair long and black. His clothes were black with brilliant flashes of gold everywhere. All of these features imprinted themselves so deeply in me that I don't think I will ever forget the magnificent image that they left in my mind. In his hands he held a regal gold shield, his wrists enclosed in gold metal cuffs. The skirt of his tunic was short pleated with plated armor encasing his chest and waist. At this time, his wings were pointed down in a relaxed position. He stood with his legs apart. Crowning this incredible apparition was his immense sword, which was held high and pointing resolutely upward.

Demons of all shapes and sizes had noticed his presence as well. They madly scurried under vehicles and over fences in order to flee him as quick as possible. You could tell by their demeanor that they were petrified, and I mean deadly petrified, by what was occurring. Even the blood-curdling, howling hellhound sprinted down the street. *(James 2:19 "You believe that there is one God. Good! Even the demons believe that—and shudder.")* As I looked on, I couldn't believe what I was witnessing. I was mesmerized by this scene. At first, I thought that I was dreaming. I quickly realized that I was wide awake and that what I was seeing was as real as real could be. Having settled into a state of prayer that was deeper than any I had ever experienced, I felt that I was right there alongside the Archangel Michael as he battled the demons!

When all of the demons had been vanquished and dispatched back to hell, my angelic protector tipped his head back, opened his mouth and released a supernatural warrior's victory roar! The sound of it was nothing short of deafening. It was accompanied by the stretching out of his snow-white wings, moving upwards above his shoulders, to a distance of approximately 15 feet on either side of his back.

To call it magnificent would hardly be doing it justice!

And then it happened as suddenly as it had begun. The roar faded as did the vision I had been witnessing. I was back in my living room, on my knees in deep prayer. Immediately I felt a heavy weight on my back that was substantial enough to cause me to stop breathing, a weight accompanied by an unbelievably sharp pain. For a moment, time froze and I found myself unable to move. Then suddenly the entire room was bathed in a bright golden light. The pain evaporated instantly, and as I recharged myself with a deep breath, I was engulfed by the most intense feeling of love. Indeed, God was protecting me through the intercession of the Archangel Michael who God sent to vanquish whatever demon had traveled over the miles from my niece's house to do me bodily harm. Again, Michael cast that demon right back into Hell from whence it sprang. Still on my knees, I felt the spirit of God so strong that I broke down and sobbed. I still sob to this day every time I think about the love and protection.

The following morning, Sidekick came downstairs and made the following statement: "Something is wrong and different in this house."

You think!

After this unbelievable victory over these unspeakably dark forces, my sister was able to enjoy a brief and wonderful period of peace. I say "brief" because it only lasted two weeks, whereupon a new detachment of demons, stronger and even more determined than ever to destroy her, invaded her home. At that point, our minds were virtual beehives swarming with question after question. How did this happen? What had introduced the new set of demons into the house? My sister and I were utterly perplexed, having only questions and no answers.

DEMON BLOCK

Just after I finished writing for the day, I went into the pantry to start dinner. Just then, a bottle of my keto MCT oil came hurling off the shelf and out the pantry door, hitting the kitchen floor and breaking in half. My brother-in-law and I were shocked!

R ight now, my head is like an L.A. freeway inter-
change at rush hour. It's an endless jumble of
thoughts going "round and round." The most insistent ones have to do with my daughter. You see, I absolutely, positively adore her, and that is precisely what makes
this so completely devastating for me. The following events

confirmed the suspicions that I've been having these past few months, suspicions which have everything to do with her situation.

With Sidekick being furious over Archangel Michael clearing out all his buddies, the tension in the house was going from bad to worse at an alarming rate. Thanks to the presence of Sidekick, I was walking on eggshells. His meltdowns were not only happening more frequently, but more openly too. As explained earlier, I was his favorite target. His deep-seated anger was invariably centered on my faith in God, and it gave rise to repeated verbal attacks against me. These attacks came fast, furiously and without warning, and they eventually became unacceptable. At one point, in fact, I began to lock myself in my room on a daily basis, having become too frightened to even venture out for a quick cup of coffee. To make it even worse, my dear husband, my earthly rock and protector, wasn't quite performing that role to the best of his ability. Every time I tried to fill him in on what was going on, his response typically amounted to something along the lines of, "He's never acted that way in front of me before".

I couldn't even begin to wrap my head around it. I mean really, what exactly was he saying? Did he think I was making it up or shamelessly embellishing the situation? What happened to my loving, protective man? Where did he go? It turned out my lack of comprehension regarding his apparent lack of concern rested on this: The "Demonic Fog." (It might help you to get a better grasp on the situation by pondering the lyrics of the

Eagles hit song "Already Gone": *you can see the sky but still not see the light.)*

This state of affairs went on for at least three months, during which time I could not count on the undivided support of either my husband or my daughter. As far as lifelines go, that left only my sister. At least she understood what I was up against. After what she had experienced her first week here, there was no question of her doubting what I was experiencing. She totally believed me (thank you, Jesus)!

Then something happened, something that as foul as it was, provided answers to the questions we were burdened with. It was late at night, probably around 2:30 am. I was sound asleep, which was pretty unusual for me during that particular stretch of night. I was abruptly awakened by something repeatedly hitting my right hip really hard. I woke up to see a tall solid black shadow man standing right by my bed, swinging its fists at me!

What the hell and what to do? Fight back!

I started swinging my fists right back at it! Yes, I was in a physical fight with a demon, a fight that left me feeling like I was in a battle for my life! I quickly moved closer to him so that I could kick my legs straight out at its torso. I realize this is crazy stuff but wait, it gets even crazier. Even though I couldn't feel my blows hitting its body, I did see it fall backwards when I managed to get one good, solid kick in its midsection with the full force of both of my legs. Then came the craziest part: I could see and feel Sidekick's presence in the demon! As difficult as it is to describe what was there, simply because it's so unbelievable, I will try my best, nonetheless. Sidekick's essence was right there in that demon, his form entering and exiting the ghoulish creature as if he were controlling it, as well as controlling the action that was taking place in my bedroom.

Eureka!

At long last, my Eureka moment was here. Sidekick was the demon, and the demon was Sidekick. Technically speaking, to be more precise, Sidekick was using the demon as a weapon in an all-out attack against me. On the floor by this time, and completely horrified by this realization, all I could think of doing at this point was to cry out for help. And then another surprise came, and this time it was a good one. No sooner had my one-word cry . . . " Jesus!" . . . escaped my lips, they both vanished in a flash. I peeked over my shoulder and saw my husband in bed. Naturally my first thought was that not even he, one of the soundest sleepers on the planet, could have possibly slept through all that commotion. I assumed wrong. My dear husband was dead to the world, as asleep as asleep can be. A bear in winter.

Note to reader. This is another trick used by demons. My sister has experienced the same problem with her husband during an attack. We believe it is possible that the demons place a partner under a specific spell, so they are oblivious.

I don't think I can summon up the words to describe the HATE I felt emanating from the demon duo: Sidekick and his demon sidekick. I am not new to this; I have felt the chillingly dark and negative energy that belongs to demons on more than one occasion in my life. This, however, was altogether different in its sheer vileness and intensity, my faith being an obvious threat to him and his minions. Sidekick, to say the least, did not enjoy me calling on God. After the encounter was finished, I made a regrettable decision to adopt an attitude of "bring it on!" (Did I mention before what an idiot I am?!)

I was able, in any case, to gain valuable insight from that whirlwind of horror. I realized in a blink of an eye why our many attempts at spiritual house cleansings had not only failed but had, at the same time, given an even tougher and more resilient group of demons the opportunity to replace the first bunch. I had even more insight into the ritualistic noises being performed upstairs in the middle of the night.

OMG! Sidekick was worshiping and working for the wrong side: Satan!

Enlightenment aside, I was left in an even more acute state of distress. Adrenaline pulsated throughout my arteries, and my blood pressure soared. There would be no sleep for me that night, for like a general whose forces are threatened with annihilation I had no choice but to stay awake until I figured out my next move. My first thought was of my sister. Should I call her and share the good news about my having finally connected the dots?

Just to be considerate, I waited all night until 6:30 am to make the call. When I told her exactly what had happened during the night and of Sidekick's involvement in it, she calmly said, "I know." Again, what the hell, but at least she understood.

In our first book, *The Hauntings of Two Sisters—Shocking True Life Experiences,* my sister and I discuss our various gifts and the close bond that we share. Truly, these are defining factors in our lives. Through our psychic abilities, we know or have a vague idea a great deal of the time of what the other sister is experiencing, be it good or bad. Pam had been abruptly awakened at the exact moment that I was being attacked by the demon duo. She knew what was happening and that it was being masterminded by Satan's Sidekick, knowledge that was eventually confirmed by my dead mother from the other side. Okay, Mom, so we've gone from "Sidekick has a dark side" to "Sidekick possesses demons." Really, Mom? There's no in-between with these two realities?

Note to reader: I discussed the total vagueness surrounding messages from the dead in a previous chapter.

This was the last time I was attacked by demons and Sidekick so directly and physically. Their next move was to regroup and employ a new agenda to harm me, and it was a whopper!

DEMON BLOCK

I was alone in the house writing this chapter when all of a sudden, I felt an extreme heavy-duty evil energy creep up behind me; a presence straight from the evil zone. This "Thing" was informing me that it was going to slam my head right into the computer keyboard! I lost no time texting my sister with an S.O.S appeal. Crazily enough, she immediately called me to let me know that they were doing the exact same thing to her. We were both having the same reaction to the energy: dizziness, nausea and pain in the back of our heads.

6

To Catch
a Thief

✝

Karen Pena

My sister, Pam, was awakened in the middle of the night by a familiar voice repeatedly screaming my name out loud: "Karen, Karen, Karen!" Immediately recognizing it as the voice of my dead father, she shot up in bed and did her best to make out what he was saying. Apparently, though, he was so upset and agitated that when he began to describe the reason for his midnight visit, she couldn't understand a word, but she definitely came away with the feeling something was terribly wrong, and it centered around me!

My father passed away 13 years ago; we hear from him so rarely. So, when he tried to make contact with her from the other side, it freaked my sister out completely. She called me very early the next morning, and after explaining what had occurred, she bombarded me with question after question. As hard as I worked at trying to calm her fears—"Pam nothing is wrong, everything is fine"—I knew darn well that my father would not have made that enormous effort if everything was fine.

Something was wrong . . . very wrong.

This occurred exactly two days before I did find out what my father was talking about and why he was so upset and agitated.

I am a very trusting person. I automatically give people that trust until it is no longer deserved, a trait that drives my poor husband crazy since he is just the opposite. He is an "earn it first" type of guy. Although this habit has caused me much emotional distress; I have always thought, nonetheless, that believing the best of people is the right approach for a Christian. As a result, for the first three months I lived in my daughter's house, I would always leave my bedroom door wide open whenever I left the house. This allowed my dog to go in and out of our bedroom when he wanted to. He loved laying on my bed to sleep. Because I am such a trusting person, I never thought anything of it. Why would I? It was my home. Clueless, absolutely clueless.

My belief system works just fine when I'm surrounded by good people but can be quite devastating when this isn't the case. After the Sidekick/demon attack in the last chapter, even though I was well aware of the fact that I was dealing with an extremely bad person in Sidekick, a Satan worshiper, I failed to connect the dots. My trust was not safe. (*Note:* I should point out, in my own defense, that The Demonic Fog, #1 on Top Ten List, was already slowly settling over me and starting to call the shots in my daily life).

Because of a terrible accident at age 14, my spine and neck were severely compromised. While out on a double date, the car we were in drove off a cliff. Over the years, the resulting back problems I suffered had triggered fibromyalgia. For the previous 18 years, I had been under the care of a pain doctor who had me taking 135 milligrams of morphine per day. Two days after my father had visited my sister, I went into my room to take my midday dose and discovered that the morphine bottle was empty! An OMG moment indeed!

If it's even possible, the situation became worse! Just then my sister called me and told me to check my jewelry, specifically, the jewelry my mother had left me. My dead mom had told my sister exactly what pieces Sidekick had taken. Immediately I checked out my jewelry chest. I discovered that the beautiful grey pearl necklace and earrings that my mother had left me, along with a necklace that my sister had given me a few months earlier for my 60th birthday, were gone! I was utterly devastated by what I had just discovered and overwhelmed by the unmitigated gall behind my daughter's boyfriend's actions. My mother's message wasn't the only evidence pointing in his direction. The simple fact of the matter was this: the only person in the house at that time who could have possibly stolen my medicine and jewelry was Sidekick! Let me repeat this last statement: Sidekick was the only one in the house who could have stolen my things! There was no evidence of a break in and no one, with the exception of the four of us, had been in the house for weeks. There was additional proof. We had a security system and a Ring with a camera attached to our front door. Since my daughter and my husband were both at work all day, only Sidekick and I were in the house during the day. Anyone else would have shown up on security cameras, and of course, nobody did.

The first issue I needed to deal with urgently was my morphine. My prescription is refilled once a month. If I lose it or someone steals it, the pain doctor does not care, for obvious reasons. Absolutely no early refills. Since I had an entire ten days to go before my prescription was due for renewal, horrible withdrawals were on the horizon for me. It became difficult to wrap my head around that prospect, as anybody who has been on opioids for an extended amount of time knows that opioids themselves create pain, a formidable double whammy.

It began almost immediately. I am here to inform you the opioid withdrawal process is just like in the movies. My skin was crawling, the pain was excruciating; I was vomiting and sweating profusely. My entire body shook without stopping and sleep was nowhere to be found. Where did that leave me? I will tell you! Walking the house in that physical state almost 24/7 for an entire week with only the lousy demons for company. Again, the question wound itself around and around in an infinite loop in my extremely unsettled brain. What kind of person is wicked enough to steal someone else's much needed pain medicine? Someone worshiping the dark side, of course. During those long nights, an epiphany came to me. It was time for me to quit taking the morphine. The last thing I could afford, in this situation, was to be vulnerable. I could not allow Sidekick and his minions to have that type of power over me. September 1, 2019, I quit opioids for good! A "WOW" moment in my life.

The second issue was my stolen jewelry.

The next morning in the backyard me, my sister Pam and our friend Aileen got into a heated discussion of the jewelry theft on the phone. All of a sudden, mom dropped in from the other side and contributed a piece that was crucial for the solving of this puzzle. She revealed to me that some of the missing jewelry could be found right there in the garage. Okay, now we're getting somewhere! After informing Pam and Aileen of the positive news, I went into the garage and started moving boxes around, intent on looking for the jewelry that had so much meaning for me. I put Pam and Aileen on speakerphone in order to free up my hands, and the three of us decided on a code phrase "Aileen, I know you have an appointment" I would use if

Sidekick came into the garage to light up a joint. Plain and simple, we were on a serious mission to find that jewelry. Thirty minutes later, Sidekick entered the garage. I wasted no time in voicing our code phrase. As soon as the words were out of my mouth, though, Aileen responded with "What appointment? I don't have an appointment!" After a few seconds of dead silence on the phone, Pam and I started laughing uncontrollably. Aileen has a wonderful deep throaty laugh. When she finally caught onto her mistake, she joined in. A truly hilarious moment! We desperately needed the comic relief. Meanwhile Sidekick, staring at me as if I were crazy, said "Can I help you look for something? I'll be happy to move the boxes for you if you'd like." Well, that quickly shut the three of us up. What the Hell? I knew by the smirk on his face he was fully aware of what we were trying to find.

I did let Sidekick help me return all boxes to their rightful place. After all, he was the reason I was in this predicament in the first place and I might as well use him for the heavy work.

But how did he know? This question was driving Pam and me crazy! Did his minions tell him what we were up to in the garage? Having heard messages ourselves from the other side, we knew just how vague and almost incomprehensible the messages can be at times. How was Sidekick privy to so many facts and details? Just then I remembered my daughter telling me, "Karen, he can hear you on the phone!" How was that possible? Every time I would talk to Aileen or Pam I spoke at a near-whisper in the backyard, garage or my downstairs bedroom. What's more, when I was on the phone with those two, Sidekick was always upstairs in the master bedroom. He'd be sleeping, playing video games or watching TV (yes, you got it, he did not have a job). But he was always far out of hearing range even if I'd been talking at a normal volume. Frantically, I tried to explain how careful I was to my daughter, but she didn't believe me. Again, I was the crazy one.

Of course, my husband did nothing about the theft and said nothing to Sidekick. He pretty much ignored it except to put a lock on our bedroom door. I also insisted he buy a camera for our bedroom that was motion activated. My hubby and I had given up our power over the situation with Sidekick concerning our daughter from day one. She asked us to let her deal with it, and trusting her as much as we did, we abided. What a mistake! It was left to me to tell Sidekick that some of my jewelry and medications were missing, that everyone needed to be on alert in the house because there may be an intruder. But, in my ear, my dead mom was screaming at me that Sidekick had committed the robbery and would do it again.

However, we never accused Sidekick of stealing my jewelry and drugs, at least not to his face. Again, how did he know? However, you would never know by his reaction. Somehow it was twisted that he stole the jewelry to pay for a meth addiction. My daughter went so far as to purchase a narcotic test for Sidekick. Please keep in mind this guy smokes dope a dozen times a day or more for his supposed PTSD which supposedly came from the aftermath of a rough childhood. The funny thing was that the test she showed me was negative, not even showing marijuana. Let's just say I don't think it was Sidekick's urine! No one was acting as if they believed he had done the stealing, meaning my daughter and husband. At that point, my daughter was in such a demonic fog that I barely recognized her energy anymore. Unfortunately, my husband wasn't far behind her. Sidekick hadn't worked since moving in with my daughter months before, so how was he buying all of his dope anyway?

Are you starting to understand what a pile of crap this was, with Sidekick becoming the victim and me the crazy bad guy? Again, what the hell? That's why we felt that we just had to give "The Demonic Fog" the #1 spot on our Top Ten List. It can completely alter your relationship with reality. By this time, almost all of us had fallen prey to complacency regarding Sidekick's reality. Thank God my sister had not succumbed and was therefore able to bring me back to an undistorted sense of reality. This was something she did during our daily morning phone conversations by letting me have it right between the eyes with "You are in a hell of a fog, Karen!"

There are no words to describe how crucial her support for me was in those very dark days. No words to describe how much her belief in me meant. She did not think I was crazy.

My sister's frustration was building! She could not believe no one was doing anything concerning Sidekick and, more importantly, that no one was believing me. To her it was unconscionable that my daughter and husband would go to work every day leaving me home with this loser! A guy who was smoking dope all day, not working and having several severe weekly meltdowns. Now on top of everything else, he was stealing from me. She couldn't believe my husband was not handling the situation and protecting me. There was one time she sat down with my husband and I to talk about the seriousness of the situation. He told her he did not believe in demons. She replied to him, "Take the demons out of it! He is an addict, having severe weekly meltdowns, breaking things throughout the house, and now stealing! You need to do something. This is common sense!" Sadly, my husband did not agree with her.

I will end this chapter, though, on a positive note. My dead mom kept telling Pam that some of her jewelry was in my old bunny cage in the garage. Yes, for once that was specific and useful information. I found her carved ivory necklace and earrings in the rabbit cage. Hallelujah!

I Am Dying
and I Know It

✝

Karen Pena

At last, we are at the beginning of the book where I began.

I am dying and I know it.

Sad to say, but at this moment I am the only one in the house that is aware of this fact. You see, both my husband and daughter have been held incommunicado, I believe, in a sort of supernatural fog by the demons that have been haunting me mercilessly for the last several months. I call it the "Demonic Fog," (#1 on our Top Ten List) and I only have become aware of this entity recently.

In essence, I am in a battlefield; at this point I am afraid that my armies are on the losing end of every encounter. My face is ravaged by deep sores and my legs are so thin that my bones, from ankle to high hip, are clearly visible. In the past 60 days I have lost close to 30 pounds, and as the vomiting and diarrhea continue without relief on an hourly basis, the weight loss continues unabated. Too weak to leave my bed, let alone make it to the ER on my own, my repeated attempts to make it clear to my husband that I was extremely ill were foiled by the Demonic Fog that had all but imprisoned him. The result is that my tearful pleading is being met with dead eyes and an utter lack of comprehension.

I fear that my already severe diabetes will be made even worse by the inability to keep any of my medications down; an outcome made even more likely by the vomiting and diarrhea-induced stress that have invaded my body. My sugars are completely out of control and I am now in a state of ketoacidosis. My breathing is quickly becoming shallow. All this adds up to the last straw for my sister, Pam, who lives in California. She calls an ambulance and then my husband.

My husband met me at the hospital just as my ambulance arrived. (My sister shares what happened next in the following chapter "Go Get Your Sister.") There really are no words to describe how much this experience opened me up to the realization that the demons could affect more than just me and my own personal space (Chapter 8 explores this realization in depth). They could carry out their agenda and activate their network of influence in an infinite ocean of complexity and ruin. Bottom line: the doctor sent me home in the exact same condition that I arrived in the ambulance, with sugars over 500 and no insulin to bring them under control.

The second I entered the house from the hospital, I immediately knew that my life had changed for the worse. For months, Sidekick and I had been engaged in a warped version of a cat-and-mouse game. My going to the hospital had only upped the ante for him and served to strengthen his resolve to keep this evil charade going. Looking back with the hindsight made possible by the passage of over a year and a half, I am convinced now that his minions were lustily screaming with joy over how near I was to death. They believed they were close to victory. So close that he was confident that the time had arrived for him to close his deal with Satan.

Even now, at times I wonder what Satan's payment would have been if he had succeeded. What was the going rate of reward for a Satan worshiper who kills a long-time born-again Christian? Was he after the permanent security he needed from being on the receiving end of my daughter's love, or was he just after money and success again? The only thing that mattered to me was of a spiritual nature—namely, my daughter's soul. The battle was on, and I was willing to sacrifice my physical health and my sanity to win it. As I am writing these words, I can again feel almost every bit of the anger and frustration that had overtaken my life. Nevertheless, I fought on, determined to see that son-of-a-bitch fail! Because after all, if he could step it up a notch so could I. God was in it to win it!

That night's torture was by far the most sadistic I had experienced to date. It was worse than the physical altercation I'd gotten into with Sidekick and his right-handed demon. Even though I knew it was coming, it still made me struggle for every breath while tearing through my world at warp speed. I walked the house all through the night, surrounded by an entourage of laughing, mocking demons who reveled in making fun of my misery. In my mind's eye I kept seeing my daughter's face, and each time I did, my heart ached with love for her and worry over the situation. My body was weak, and the pain had intensified to the point where I could barely breathe. My face was washed by tears on a regular basis, and I cried out to God to help me over and over again as I lay in bed in the wee hours. I now relied on Him all the more fervently since looking to my husband or my beloved daughter for support was useless. They were out of it, so to speak, their ability to size up the situation accurately thwarted by the Demonic Fog in which they were imprisoned. Truthfully, honestly, they thought I was just plain crazy!

On one particular night, I went out into the backyard for a smoke and some much-needed relief. Lo and behold, who was right there beside me but the Smoking Demon himself. He came up with at least 10 different malignant and horrible scenarios in which I could end my life and misery. By around 2:30 am, just as the jumble of thoughts that were slipping and sliding around in my head were beginning to lead me to agree with him that suicide was the only answer, my phone rang. What the hell? It was my sister.

My dead mother had woken her up from a deep sleep, pleading with her to call me immediately unless she was prepared to see me lose it completely. Again, it was Mom to the rescue from the other side.

I shared everything that happened that night with my sister. We talked for a long time and even though I never did get any of the R & R I so badly needed that night, a crisis was avoided, and a major victory was won! The minions were never able to mentally drive me to that hideous dark place again. The following morning, I made a promise to myself: I would not smoke from 6:00 pm until 6:00 am. A promise which, to my credit, I was able to keep.

A week later, I was cooking in the kitchen when I happened to glance up and saw Sidekick standing at the top of the stairs. What happened next was nothing short of mind boggling. All of a sudden, Sidekick came tumbling down the stairs and landed flat on his back in the living room! He immediately lifted his head and, with a laser-like focus, aimed a long, ice cold stare at me. I believe that in the ensuing silence we were both processing what had just occurred. Sidekick was in shock from the fall, and I was in shock also but for a profoundly different reason. I had seen a pair of arms and hands shove hard against his upper back at the top of the stairs. When I saw that he had gotten his breath back, I asked Sidekick for his version of what had just happened. His reply was he had tripped on his big toe.

What the hell? Another lie, another game. He had to know that he was violently pushed from behind. He was determined not to give me the satisfaction of knowing something from the other side had attacked him. What he didn't know is that I knew even more than he did about what had just happened. What I knew was that the Something Good had come to my aid via the cooperation of my dead father and father-in-law. No guesswork was necessary on my part. I had seen their ghosts at the top of the stairs just before Sidekick went flying. My father's exact words were, "You're going to f__k with my daughters? Then I'm going to f__k with you!" Evidently, the two of them, my father and father-in-law, did not push Sidekick hard enough. Not only did he survive, he now knew that spirits on the other side were protecting me. This bit of knowledge on his part was crucial, so crucial that it eventually became a big problem for him and, ultimately, for me as well.

I chose to not put much effort into familiarizing myself with Sidekick's rituals. I chose instead to keep my eyes and heart on God. One thing I did not doubt is that Sidekick did have power; power that came from Satan. During the numerous talks I've had with him about God, I reminded him repeatedly that Satan is not a god. He is a fallen angel who only has as much power as God allows him. *(Revelation 12:9 "So the great dragon was cast out, that serpent of old, called the Devil and Satan, who deceives the whole world, he was cast to the earth, and his angels were cast out with him.") (John 19:11 "Jesus answered Satan, 'You would have no power at all against Me unless it had been given you from above.')*

At this point, rather than return the favor and push me down the stairs on the occasions I went up, the Satanic minions would shoulder check me instead. For the first time in 33 years, my husband was on laundry duty. I was spared the horror of running their ghoulish gauntlet. Okay, I must make a confession here. I lied in order to spare myself further punishment. I knew they couldn't wait to send me tumbling down those stairs like Sidekick. So, I told him my bad knee made it excruciatingly painful for me to drag my body up and down the stairs. As part of my demon-evasion plan, I even stopped going upstairs to use our computer. Eventually, we made a small office in my downstairs bedroom and put the computer in it. Between all the things we had to do and the little games we had to play to avoid this demonic harassment, it was exhausting trying to stay ahead of them. I kept telling myself, "Stay alive for Jennifer!"

The vomiting, diarrhea and pain became more serious by the week, continuing on a nonstop basis day after day and night after night. Since I still couldn't keep down my diabetic medicine, my sugars were running around 400-600 daily. Then my bowels succumbed. Everything had turned a deep shade of black and I could not hold it in any longer. All I could think was, "What the hell now?" In our first book, *The Hauntings of Two Sisters—Shocking True Life Experiences*, we talk about my grandmother sitting at the edge of a bed when a loved one was ready to pass. My grandmother was coming to the side of my bed every night. She was enveloping my arm or face with a touch of her supernatural heat and love. I soon realized that she and Mom were taking turns. One would keep vigil next to me while the other would fight to keep the demons out of my room. My sister was still doing her part, calling every morning and making me laugh by inquiring if grandma had been sitting on the edge of my bed the night before. When I told her no, that she was actually at the side of my bed, Pam would give a huge sigh of relief.

Now is as good a time as any to address the guilt I was feeling back then. This is anything but what I wanted for my loved ones' afterlife. I believe that when a soul enters Heaven, there is a huge celebration. I very much wanted my mom and grandmother to enjoy celebrating with joy and love. Instead, they were stuck down here on earth in a demon-infested house, Hell's sublet. Both were trying their best to save me because I hadn't listened to my dead mother's warning about Sidekick's dark side. The love and support they showed me is really what kept me going through those infernally bleak nights.

Over the next two weeks, I became so ill that I was unable to get out of bed except to crawl to the bathroom. This was a journey I couldn't make at times since my life force was so weak it was almost non-existent. No one noticed, understood or cared, and I was done talking, asking and/or begging for help! Then one morning my sister called. . . .

8

Go Get
Your Sister

✝

Pam Mandel

My sister was dying.

Over the past three months she'd become sicker and sicker! Despite her desperate attempts for help from her family, no one in her household had yet to step in. She was getting weaker and weaker by the day and her weight was dropping fast, too fast. Not being able to hold down food or liquids, not even water, was taking its toll on her body. As scary as that was, having the minions surrounding her 24/7 was slowly taking away her will to live. She was just too sick to care, too sick to fight. "Disastrous Agendas for Victims" (#4 on our Top Ten List) There was 600 miles of hard road separating us, and I felt totally helpless. After reaching out for weeks to her husband and daughter to make them aware of my concerns, it had become obvious to me that they couldn't comprehend the urgency of the situation.

The clincher came in the form of a distress call from Karen.

Her voice was so weak, I had to work extra hard to make out what she was trying to tell me. She had reached the point where she was so badly paralyzed by nausea that she couldn't even get out of bed to go to the bathroom. Frantically, I called 911 from my home just east of San Francisco only to be asked to wait patiently while they transferred me to the nearest fire station in Las Vegas. WTH! Twenty minutes later, the ambulance finally arrived at my sister's home. I then dialed her husband at work to make him aware of her current situation. He left work in time to meet the ambulance at the emergency room.

After the completion of several tests, the only problem the doctor could find was her blood sugar level, which had reached a dangerously high count of over 500. Her inability to keep anything down meant she was being deprived of the helpful benefits of her diabetic medication. She desperately needed insulin shots to bring her sugar level down to a safe number. To make matters even worse, after this life-threatening emergency the doctor literally sent her home in the exact same condition that she was in when the ambulance arrived. Again, it only served to once again make her look crazy.

Strangely enough, my own experience as a serious diabetic led me to believe that she must be going into Diabetic Ketoacidosis (DKA). However, her blood test read negative in that department! With all the trouble she was having just breathing, besides her severe diarrhea and flu-like aches and pains—and let's not forget the awful vomiting— I had to seriously doubt the results of the test. I remained firmly convinced that she was showing all of the classic symptoms of DKA. Then, in a flash, this strange and extremely distressing sequence of events gave way to a thought. Although having come straight out of left field, it seemed to make perfect sense. I am talking about the #1 on our Top Ten List: The Demonic Fog. It seems that the Fog had struck again tonight. This time it had done its work not only on my sister's daughter and husband but on the doctor as well. I have been a severe diabetic for decades and there is no way to explain how bizarre this ER doctor's behavior was. My sister should have been immediately admitted and kept in the hospital until her sugars were stabilized. To me this was outrageous!

The 600 miles that separated my sister and I left me feeling so frustrated and hopeless that my first impulse was to drop everything, drive to Las Vegas, toss her in the back seat of our truck and take her home with me. There was, however, one huge issue that had kept me from doing this so far: my fear of a repeat performance of what I had gone through back in February during my first visit to her house. Although my sister had spent many hours trying to talk me through the fear, I just couldn't help myself! The fact of the matter was that I was so shaken up by what I had gone through that I just didn't know if I could bring myself to even set foot in Hell's sublet again.

The fear I'd felt during that first visit was overwhelming. Every day I would watch with dread as the clock ticked its way towards dark. The anxiety that I felt with each tick was so overwhelming that it had made me physically ill. The horror I experienced on a nightly basis had emblazoned itself so deeply on my consciousness that nothing on this earth could begin to convince me to consider going through that nightmare again. That being said, however, what were my options? I knew that this time it was a matter of life and death for my one and only sister.

So, it took something not of this earth to change my mind. I was woken up abruptly one night by my dead mother telling me to get off my frightened ass and go get my sister now! After hearing the strained emotion in her voice, I decided that this was definitely a case of mother-knows-best.

I called my sister that morning to tell her of my decision.

This time, however, I was going to play it smart. To avoid being alone upstairs in my sister's house, I would bring my husband, my protector, with me. I prayed for God's blessing and soon we were on the road. Since this decision was made a week before Thanksgiving, guess where we were spending Thanksgiving—in Las Vegas with my sister and her family. Hopefully, we would have a warm holiday reunion with plenty of TLC without party crashers from the nether world! A wonderful thought that had no basis in reality. Bottom line: We were on our way to Hell's sublet!

After nine hours of driving with our two dogs, we finally arrived at my sister's. When I stepped into the house, a surprise awaited me in the form of an atmosphere so heavy with demonic depression, oppression and possession that I sucked in my breath. The very thing I'd dreaded was here in spades. I just knew it was going to be a week of spiritual nightmares and more. And then an even worse shock revealed itself to me. As bad as my sister's condition was the last time I had visited her, this time it was even worse— much worse. My mom was absolutely right to tell me to get my ass down here and get it down here fast! My sister looked awful. Her skin was hanging off her, her eyes were gaunt and hollowed-out. She was covered in sores and her coloring ranged from just grey to bordering on lifeless. As if all that weren't bad enough, she must have lost over 30 pounds! Normally this would be a good thing but as fast as she lost it, she looked so ill, fragile, vulnerable. My God, exactly what had Sidekick and his minions done to her?

Again, the question was bouncing around in my badly overworked brain. How could my dear sister's husband and daughter, living under the same roof with her decomposing day after day, not see what was happening to her?

It just had to be the "The Demonic Fog"!

They weren't seeing real reality.

Not living in a house surrounded by demons and rituals 24/7, I was not a prisoner of this fog. So, by process of elimination if for no other reason, I was the supernatural "911" for this infestation from Hell. Fortunately, my mind was clear and ready for the assignment. God let me know exactly what I needed to do: save Karen's life by bringing her home with me. It was right then and there, with this Eureka moment, that the fear of being in that house left me. I had bigger fish to fry so I decided that once was enough. I was not going to let these demonic terrors torture me a second time. With this morale-boosting certainty, I felt the love of God's strength flow through me. This time I just knew that by God's saving grace I was finally ready for them to "bring it on!"

By this stage of the game, I knew exactly what was transpiring in that house. It was crystal clear to me that Sidekick and his minions had indeed pulled out all the stops and simply wanted her dead ASAP. Her psychic gifts and her deep, abiding love of God were getting in the way of whatever agenda they had in store. I was ready, however, for whatever was to come, as I felt totally protected by God and by my protecting husband. I was wrong.

The very first night, as I left my room and turned into the hall on my way to the bathroom, I was treated to a growl deeper than any I'd ever heard. There, not more than two feet away from me, was a very, very large dog. Hello, Hellhound! I locked eyes with him, and unphased by neither the savage glare coming from those hellish yellow peepers nor the less than amicable energy that was rolling off him in great big waves, I greeted him with the following message: "I guess you didn't get the memo! Back off, demon!!!" I even started carrying my camera around, so I'd be ready to capture a shot of them the moment I sensed their presence. I would simply point the camera in their direction, say "smile" and snap a picture. However, my newfound spirit of resolve turned out to be a mixed blessing. For although it had given me just what I needed to end their unholy hold over my poor sister, I could feel their anger at me growing apace with my new sense of fearlessness.

But you know what?

I didn't care!

Sensing that I had shifted the balance of power in my battle with them, the minions must have gotten together and had a guild meeting. It was their time to devise a new strategy, since the old one obviously was no longer working. They actually came up with a new agenda and a new direction. My failure to detect both changes proved to be devastating to my own health and well-being. The following day I saw that my immediate goal had to be to get my sister out of the house and away from the demonic oppression that had been sucking the life out of her for months. After a few days of finally being able to keep some liquids down, she was feeling slightly better. Since she seemed well enough to venture outside, we decided to take a ride and see if a change of scenery would help lift her sagging spirits. Again, I was mistaken.

My husband grew up back East eating White Castle hamburgers. They had just opened one on the Las Vegas Strip. The four of us, Michael, Karen, her husband and I jumped into the truck and headed that way. White Castle was right outside the Venetian Hotel, so we parked in their garage. At this point of the story, the important fact to remember is that my sister and her husband had been to the Venetian dozens of times during the 18 years they had lived in Las Vegas and knew the area well.

Walking through the casino, our husbands needed to use the restroom, so my sister and I sat down at the slot machines to gamble a bit while waiting for them to return. This is where the story starts getting strange. Minutes went by and still no husbands, so we ordered a pair of drinks from the waitress and continued to gamble. After another 15 minutes had gone by, we knew that something was wrong. Too much time had passed for your average pit stop, and our concern had turned into fear. After a few unanswered calls to their cellphones, we headed towards the restrooms. Still no sign of them. On the verge of panic at that point but determined to do our best to keep calm, we settled on a plan of action. We would make a complete circle of the casino floor to see if they were somewhere in that vast expanse. We proceeded to do just that. After only one round of the room's circumference, we found them looking for us. Their explanation for having disappeared—we got lost! Really? It's a circle!

Finally, with all four of us reunited, we headed to the concierge desk by the hotel's front entrance to ask how to get to White Castle. Again, we were treated to a Twilight Zone moment! The concierge told us we would need to take a taxi since we were a long way from my husband's favorite hamburger joint. WTH? We had just passed it coming into the Venetian parking lot. Things were starting to get totally weird!

Karen replied, "No worries, we have been here dozens of times and we always eat at the Grand Café. It's at the bottom of the escalators, a safe hop, skip and a jump from where we are now." So, we began walking in that direction, and after 30 minutes of searching, the Grand Café was nowhere to be found! Again, it's a circle! We inquired at one of the restaurants concerning its location and they pointed us in the direction we had just come from. Then we asked a casino floor manager and he pointed us in the opposite direction!! Again WTH??? By now, two hours have gone by since finding our husbands, two hours in which we have walked and walked that casino circle. During this time my insulin pump was giving off a steady beat of low sugar warnings. The next casino employee we asked for directions from, pointed us in yet another direction!

By now this circus of wrong directions and wasted steps was making less and less sense to us. After walking around the circle-shaped casino over and over again, my insulin pump told me that my sugar reading was at a dangerously low 47. (In perspective, 125 is normal for me) This was getting close to pass-out time for me. It was a head-scratcher. After all, I had a Bailey's cocktail earlier that evening. Why would my sugar count be that low?? Satisfying myself with an explanation that blamed the excessively low count on all the walking we had done, I announced that we needed to find a restaurant right away!

I started to cry, my mind becoming more and more confused and muddled from my low sugars. Something wasn't right! Despite the large orange juice that Michael had procured from the nearest cocktail waitress, my sugar count sank lower and lower. Again WTH? Finally, we found a restaurant! Although it wasn't a very good one, at least it gave me the opportunity to treat my seriously weakened body to some solid food. I am 63 years old and had never experienced this diabetic hazy confusion before. But to have it happen to all four of us at the same time was incomprehensible. The Demonic Fog strikes again! It's the only explanation for the way all of us had been affected— hotel staff included—all at the same time. It wasn't until the following morning that the other shoe would finally drop, and the demons' new agenda would at last become crystal clear to me.

That night I was awakened at 2:00 am by a rhythmic sound (a beat of drums perhaps) coming from the other side of the bedroom wall that had a huge walk-in closet adjoining it. Was Sidekick doing rituals?

The next morning, my sister's condition had deteriorated after the previous night's misadventure. On the other hand, I had fully recovered from my low sugar episode, or so I thought. With our husbands having headed out with the dogs for a long walk in the desert, Karen and I found ourselves home alone. At around 9:30 am, with

Karen downstairs in her bedroom resting and me in the upstairs bedroom, I started to feel funny. I looked down at the insulin pump, which also tells me my sugar levels, and saw that OMG, my sugars had started to crash. Then I noticed that within the hour the pump had just given me ten units of insulin.

Who on earth could have done that?

It certainly wasn't me!

Administering additional insulin requires pushing a series of buttons in just the right sequence and is anything but a simple task. With sugars at 57 and 9.1 units left of active insulin inside me, I was in trouble! I tried to walk but couldn't. With my husband not in the house, I had to get a hold of my sister. I tried yelling for her, but she didn't hear me. I called her on the cell phone, and, thank God, she answered. I asked her to bring me a big glass of orange juice to help me adjust my sugar levels. It was so hard for her to climb the stairs; as she did, I could hear her vomiting into her vomit bag along the way. Meanwhile, all I could do was just lie there waiting for the badly needed infusion of sugar. I was utterly confused. How did I get ten units of insulin in me? Thank God the pump's safety feature did not allow it to exceed ten units. Without that feature, who knows what would have happened.

I started to reflect on the previous night at the casino. Could the same thing have happened then? I never checked if insulin was shot into me because I hadn't done it. Did the demons give me extra insulin? I was confused by the low sugars, since having a shot of Bailey's usually sends my sugars reeling in the opposite direction. (*Note:* This, by the way, comes in at #5 on the Top Ten List under "Device/Electronics Manipulators.") Now I was positive the demons were not only trying to kill my sister, but me as well. At that point, I knew beyond a shadow of a doubt what made them tick. It was as plain as day. The one thing they absolutely did not want to happen was for me to take my sister home with me to help her get better. Literally, they were willing to kill me so that they could complete their execution of her! That is when Karen and I knew we needed to call in help. There were too many demons and not enough angels in Hell's sublet.

The next morning, Sidekick came down the stairs and asked me if he could take my Goldendoodle, Dexter, for a run in the desert. With all the energy this dog has I thought what could go wrong, so I said sure! But Dexter came back from this run acting different and it is fair to say a little skittish, something I had never seen before in him. But things started to get busy, and I didn't give it another thought. That was until the next morning when Sidekick came down the stairs and ask to take Dexter for another walk. The voice I heard from the other side was "NOOOOOO." I was shocked! But then should I really be shocked knowing what Sidekick is all about? I thought, "Really Pam, with all the hate he has towards you, why won't he take this out on the dog you love so much." Get a clue! I immediately shared this with my sister because he was always taking her dog Cash on those long runs in the desert. Was he doing some kind of ritual on them! The thought of that just made me sick to my stomach.

Sidebar: My sister did look up one ritual on animals. This one required animal blood to perform the ritual. Is this why the other side said " NOOOOOOO"? Is this why Dexter had acted strange after the walk with Sidekick?

I had to survive five more days before we left. After we did one more night at the casino, Karen became sicker than ever and unable to hold anything down, not even water. A couple nights later everyone but my sister wanted some relief from all the stress, so we settled on a game of poker. Sidekick was ecstatic. This was his game of choice and he was supposedly good at it; he immediately took charge. Halfway through the first game he became so aggressive with his bids that the rest of us decided to set a limit on betting. I looked at him and said, "You will not intimidate me." Everyone laughed, thinking I was joking around. Was I? I repeated it several times during the game, always during the bidding process. When I did, he would just look at me. I really believed he knew without a doubt that I was not talking about the poker game. He knew darn well, in fact, that I was talking about him and the despicable nightly rituals he'd engineered to cause harm to me and my family. The funny thing is my sister's daughter—Sidekick's girlfriend—began to accuse him as well. I was certain, though, that only he and I knew what my refusal to be intimidated really was all about. After that night, whenever he was sitting in the family room watching TV and I came down to join him, he would immediately get up and walk upstairs. Since this happened repeatedly, it was obvious to me that he was uncomfortable being in the same room with me. Not that I really minded, seeing that this was actually a good thing. I was as equally uncomfortable with him.

The strange thing was as I interacted with my sister's husband, whom I have known for over 35 years, that week, he was different, and not in a positive way. Whether he believed it or not, these demonic roommates of theirs, let's just say, were changing who he was. I knew then, my sister was on her own in that house. She was the crazy outsider, and I was the only one who believed her!

Finally, Thanksgiving arrived, and my husband and I were treating everyone to dinner at a nearby restaurant—everyone, that is, but my sister. As much as she tried really hard to get ready for our holiday meal, the vomiting was so bad that in the end she chose not to take a chance on it. Although we kept our reservation, we came home directly after the meal so that she wouldn't be alone long. Two days later, we packed up the truck and started back to the Bay Area with my sister in the back seat. Let's just say thank God Karen was armed with a supply of barf bags. She was sick all the way home.

It was one of the longest rides we have ever had back home from Las Vegas but nevertheless, we made it back home safely!

Pam with her husband Michael

9

Road to
Recovery

✠

Pam Mandel

My sister was exhausted after a ten-hour drive from Las Vegas to the San Francisco Bay Area. My husband and I knew we needed to take the long view of her recovery, so before we even left for Las Vegas, we were busy beavers making everything ready for her stay. The long ride would take its toll on her, and she would need a lot of down time before I could even think about starting her on the road to recovery.

Please allow me a moment to vent. Lately I've become more frustrated than ever, the tension that's engulfed us all having become so dreadful that I am having nightmares on a regular basis. They have been getting worse and worse, along with anger as I sit back and think about the dysfunctional state of my sisters' household. Sidekick is still hard at work creating total havoc there and no one is doing anything about it. I keep wondering, "What is wrong with these people?" Why haven't they kicked his ass out yet? My sister is locking herself in her room on a daily basis just to avoid his temper tantrums and attacks. I am stupefied by the fact that her husband just won't do anything to help solve the problem—so much so that I've even entertained the idea of making the 600-mile drive down there and kicking Sidekick out myself! However, not my place.

We tried to witness God to him, only to see the hatred for God ooze out of his every pore and his eyes turn black with anger. In over 60 years, I have never encountered anything like this! His negativity is so poor that the family can't even celebrate Christmas or Easter. This doesn't surprise me at all. It has been months of living in Hell's sublet. Bottom line: The nightly rituals, the sorcery he performs, the demonic attacks are really getting old, and my frustration is made steadily worse by my sister's continuing to live there with a husband who refuses to validate what she's going through. They say she's the crazy one, but I feel it's just the opposite.

At this point, I've had it. My response to Sidekick is, "Enough of the demonic activity!" Not only has he stolen much of my sister's jewelry—some which was my mom's—but his theft of her medication has resulted in a painful process of withdrawals for her and a diet of daily temper tantrums. She was totally stressed out, and as a result she became sicker and sicker.

Get a clue, hubby—move out!

Whew . . . now I feel better—we can continue!

Back to our plan. First, deal with the physical problems, then take care of the spiritual ones. This way we hoped to make Karen strong enough in both body, mind and spirit to handle herself when she returned home. First, we needed to find out what was going on with her physically. Why was she bleeding internally? Why couldn't she hold down any food or liquids? Since she was so sick and weak, I called for an ambulance and followed them to the ER. After conducting a battery of tests over a period that lasted hours, they concluded that she had a bleeding ulcer for which they prescribed three different medications. They also wanted her to have an endoscopy and colonoscopy as soon as possible. They referred her to a particular gastroenterologist and sent over the medical records for him to review. They made an appointment for the following week. I began to cheer up a bit, believing that we might be turning the corner on her health.

At least that is what I believed at the time. Then the following week, the strangest thing happened upon arriving at the gastroenterologist's office. As soon as he entered the room, he announced that my sister's only problem was her diabetes and nothing else. I couldn't believe it! After her blood work was done and the test results from the ER had been analyzed, the doctor had insisted that the endoscopy and colonoscopy be done immediately. He had referred us to this doctor because the ER wasn't equipped to perform these procedures. As hard as my sister and I tried to explain the situation again, he would not even take the time to listen. He had made up his mind and that was final. When I think back on this extremely unpleasant moment, the thing I remember most clearly is my saying to this man, "You are useless! Call my sister an ambulance immediately to take her to the ER again!" When he reminded me that the hospital was only a block away, I responded with "I don't care! She can barely walk so she needs an ambulance!" He finally asked his nurse to call the ambulance for us and they took Karen back to the ER. Another doctor in another location in another Demonic Fog? This was truly unbelievable!

Once back in the Emergency Room they were puzzled as to why the gastroenterologist didn't do what they had asked him to do. Another week had gone by and they could tell that my sister was worse off than she had been the week earlier. Now she was so dehydrated that they couldn't even find a vein to insert the IV needle. Finally, they called another nurse, and she was able to get the job done. Her body drank in the liquid, along with the desperately needed medications that were mixed in with it. After over four hours of being infused, she started to feel better. Seeing that she communicated a little more clearly, I decided that she'd begun her return to the land of the living. On that basis, I felt it was okay for me to go home, feed our dogs and then head back to the ER.

I gave my sister a warm hug and told her I would be right back. While on my way to my car, with both hands full, I was pushed from behind and fell down hard on both knees. I just laid there, contemplating what had just happened, the pain so bad that I couldn't move; I wondered if I was still alive. (Heaven had to be better than an ugly concrete parking lot.) I hit both of my knees, one elbow, and my chin on the pavement, cutting myself in several places in the process. Someone saw me fall and ran to get help, and an orderly from the ER came out with a wheelchair to aid me in returning upright.

Next thing my sister sees is me in a wheelchair being pushed into the ER all cut up. They parked the wheelchair right next to her, and I'd be hard pressed to describe the expression that appeared on her face after she had a good look at me! All she could say was, "What the hell happened to you?" Really! Actually, I was thinking the exact same thing. What did just happen to me? Who shoved me hard? Who could have possibly done it, since there was no one around!

They sent her home with several medications in hand along with instructions to follow a strict diet in order to give her bleeding ulcers time to heal. Karen researched "healing ulcers" and found a wonderful kale smoothie called "Ulcer Buster." She religiously drank the smoothie every morning. Within a couple of weeks, she was feeling much better and we were ready to move on to phase two of our healing processes—healing her spirit. One thing I was sure of: After sharing a home with a Satan worshiper and a house full of demons, my sister desperately required a good spiritual cleansing, maybe more than one. One night we invited a friend who was also an ordained minister and sensitive to come over for dinner and some fellowshipping. Although our friend has been to the house many times before, this time she got lost on her way over, so badly lost that a ride that should have taken 30 minutes lasted over an hour and a half. What was up with that? Did something or someone simply not want her to use her psychic powers that day? If so, how did Sidekick even know about her visit?

Again, this was driving my sister and me crazy!

After seeing the demons walking through my California home on several occasions, it confirmed my suspicion that Sidekick was the source. I knew he could derail my sister's healing process, a suspicion that was reinforced by Karen's admitting that she could see and feel evil lying next to her in bed, night after night. What was unmistakable was he was going through his book of Satan tricks to keep her from getting better! Knowing this, I figured that I better sleep with both ears and at least one eye open, in a manner of speaking, just in case she was attacked by something Sidekick decided to send her way. Needless to say, she was very fragile at this time.

One night around midnight I was awakened by that old

familiar feeling, a feeling that told me someone/something really, really awful was too close for comfort. Sitting up in my bed and looking around the room I saw it right away—the spitting image of Sidekick, right there in the room with me. I couldn't believe it. I immediately jumped out of bed and ran down the hall to my sister's room, where I found her being pinned by her wrists against the mattress. Whoever or whatever was holding her down, released her the moment I came through the door, leaving a bruise on her wrist that was clearly visible the next day.

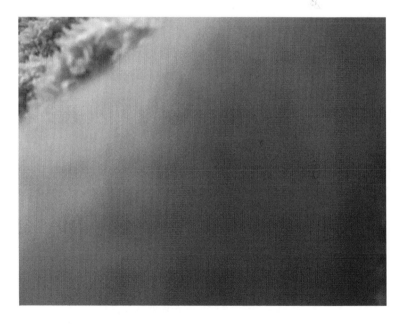

Wrist with bruise

A few nights later, I heard a commotion coming from the living room. When I logged onto my camera app to see what was going on, I thought I saw my sister's dwarf lop ear bunny, Apple, scurry across the floor and into our bedroom. Puzzled as to how Apple could have gotten out of her cage, I jumped up and started searching for her. Not seeing her in our room, I decided to try the living room. There she was, right where she belonged—in her cage with the cage door shut tight! OMG, what was it that I'd just seen hippity-hopping across the floor? As I reflected on my sighting of Ms. Bunny-from-who-knows-where, it dawned on me that this "alt-bunny" didn't have a cotton tail—but Apple did! What was the purpose of this phantom bunny?

Now that Karen was starting to feel better physically, it was time to deal with phase II: her spiritual health. Bottom line: My sister was simply not herself. She was so oppressed and depressed that there was little of her personality or life force left. I made an appointment with a Spiritual Healer. The day we went to see her, my sister was very nervous. She was very aware that thanks to Sidekick's rituals, a host of demons had attached themselves to her. She calls them demonic Velcro. As it turned out, however, what we were actually dealing with was much more than we'd even imagined! The Spiritual Healer explained to her that the demons that had attached themselves to her were of the (very powerful) Luciferic kind. What really hit home regarding the Healer's revelation was the news of health-related curses being levied against nine of her *chakras. As shocked as we were upon hearing this, it did give us, nonetheless, some badly needed new information. It in fact readily explained to a "T" the health crisis she had been experiencing for months. After the cleansing, my sister told me she felt like a new person, her life-force gradually returning as each individual chakra was cleared and blessed. She was markedly better off for the cleansing, as was demonstrated by her body's newly recovered health. After warning us that Karen was by no means out of the proverbial woods yet, the Spiritual Healer carefully explained how dangerous and powerful Sidekick had to be to show the degree of proficiency that was needed to direct a swarm of Lucifer demons at my sister. Supposedly, Lucifer-demons make up Satan's private army, performing the same role that the SS did for Hitler. Scary stuff indeed. However, now we knew exactly who and what we were up against. Well, at least we believed we did.

One morning, Karen came into the living room looking very sleepy. She said that a rhythmic "tapping" on the window had kept her up most of the night for the 3rd night in a row. When she moved back the curtain and glanced out, there was nothing there. We checked my security cameras and all we saw were some serious orbs, very large right outside her window.

Again, WTH?

Karen had made noticeable progress in getting free of the demonic fog and was able to start making plans again, foremost of which was the one that involved moving out of their daughter's home and getting a place of their own. After many discussions with her husband and decisions made, they set a date for their move: June 1, 2020. As the date came closer, unfortunately, so did the 2020 pandemic, and the move was put on hold.

My sister's health was improving in all ways as the weeks passed: mentally, physically and spiritually. A new plan was made that called her husband to drive up for the annual family Christmas party and take her back home. The day of the party arrived, and my sister was going to see her husband for the first time in over two months. I spent the day helping her get all dolled up. We both looked forward to surprising her husband with her new look, but then someone or something pushed my sister so hard from behind that it jerked her entire body. Her body was wracked in pain just before the party was supposed to begin. After Karen took several Advil we headed to the party as planned.

Again, WTH?

Her hubby arrived first at the party. On seeing Karen walk into the house a few minutes later, his face lit up with joy—a badly needed and refreshing sight after the gloom and doom vibe of those past few months. He was, to say the least, surprised; not only did she look beautiful but, more importantly, she looked healthy as well! He lost little time in letting me know how thankful he was for everything I'd done to help get her to this point. All I did, really, was guide her while she did whatever was necessary to move the healing process along.

The day after the Christmas party, they drove home to Las Vegas.

Hopefully both stronger and more spiritually equipped to handle the road ahead of her.

Chakras: In Sanskrit the word "chakra" means "disk" or "wheel" and refers to the energy centers in your body. These wheels or disks of spinning energy each correspond to certain nerve bundles and major organs. To function at their best, your chakras need to stay open, or balanced. If they get blocked, you may experience physical or emotional symptoms related to a particular chakra. The main Chakras run from the base of your spine and extend to the crown of your head.

Today I was writing "Chapter 10" when all of a sudden Microsoft Word kicked me out and asked for a password! WTH? I called my husband at work asking for the password and he said, "Are you crazy? No one puts a password on Word!" I have been trying for 30 minutes to get back in: nothing, my writing is done for the day. It took my husband two days to get our computer right again. He could not understand what had transpired.

10

Our Light
Bulb Moments

✝

Pam Mandel
& Karen Pena

Have you ever experienced a moment in time when all of a sudden, the dots start to connect? Concerning happenings in the past that you always questioned and wondered about? The why of it? During my sister's Road to Recovery period, we spent a lot of time reflecting on our current situation surrounding Sidekick. Karen and I began to talk about the numerous visitations he made to our homes over the past 20 years. My light bulb moment went off the day I helped move my sister into her daughter's new home. Seeing that demon walking across the living room floor just after ten minutes in the house followed by the week of nightly horrors, was too much of a coincidence for me!

As Karen and I continued to discuss Sidekick's visitations through the weeks, another light bulb went off. I heard our dead mother from the other side yell the name of the street my sister lived on when they first moved to Las Vegas. I immediately told my sister and wow did her light bulb moment happened!

Below are the two stories of our light bulb moments after Sidekick had stayed in our homes. This comes under "Revenge/Retaliation" (#3 of our Top Ten List).

PAM'S STORY

In all my years of seeing things from the other side I had never seen a demon before Sidekick stayed with my husband and me over 18 years ago. When my sister moved to Las Vegas, her daughter would come back to visit and see her friend Sidekick. She would stay with us and he would come visit her during the day while my husband and I were at work. She would probably visit every three months and stay several days at a time.

During that period after living years with no demons or negative entities, things soon started to change.

I started to feel a strange and uneasy sensation when I would come home from work, open the front door and turn the lights on. At first it didn't happen every day, just occasionally. But then it started to escalate. I began to pay more attention, and I mean a lot more attention, to this feeling. Chalking it up to the wind, dogs, or just the house settling no longer made sense. I just knew beyond a doubt that there was a negative energy in the house hiding somewhere. The first time I felt it, I let our dogs in and watched them very carefully to see if they were guided with that celebrated doggie ESP to a particular place in the house. It was business as usual for them, however. The only object of their attention, as always, was mommy, who was greeted with the usual burst of excitement reserved for parental homecomings. At that point I decided to roll up my sleeves and get to work on cracking this case. I initiated a daily routine of inspecting every room and closet (and even the showers) to check for the intruder that I just knew was there. Not knowing or even giving it any thought as to what I would do if I ever found an intruder! The results of that surveillance were always zero, and I just chalked it all up to my imagination.

A few months later, we went to Hawaii on a planned vacation. We left my girlfriend's son in charge of watching the family home for us. On the second night away, we received a frantic call from him telling us that he felt someone's presence in the house. We told him to do an inspection tour while we stayed on the phone with him. Searching every nook and cranny, he found nothing or no one. That still did not satisfy him, and his fear continued to grow along with his conviction that someone or something was keeping him company! Concerned about his emotional state, we called a friend and asked him to come over to check things out and spend some time with him until he felt comfortable again. It apparently worked, and there were no further distress calls from him while we were away on vacation.

It was, however, by no means over. When we returned back from our vacation this feeling of someone being in the house began to happen on a daily basis.

The mood in our home began to change, as did the nitty gritty of daily life. It seemed that between us there were more and more arguments, and simple disagreements often intensified into dramatic fights. There was a depressed feeling throughout our home. Emotions were on high alert, and in the meantime, something had - at least temporarily - cancelled the love, laughter and happiness that had been in our lives.

And then things really began to escalate, with shadows in our peripheral vision, figures in the dark, footsteps, noises, knocking sounds, doors slamming and that constant feeling that someone was watching us. My husband would say, "I thought (our son) was out tonight."

"He is," I would reply.

"Well, I just saw him come down the stairs so he must have come home."

We would check out the entire house, only to find that there was no one home but us. I asked him what exactly had he seen? He would tell me he saw a tall shadow out of the corner of his eye. A few days later both my son and I started to see this shadow. I saw it mostly coming down the staircase. It was always out of the corner of our eye, and that led us to question ourselves. Did we really see it or was it just the lighting playing tricks on our vision? Maybe, in fact, it was just my imagination succumbing to fear and fatigue. One thing that was beyond a reasonable doubt, in any case, was that this whole thing was getting weirder and creepier by the minute! I hated being home. The home we spent so much time remodeling and making just the way we wanted, terrified me! Several times the feeling was so strong that I asked my husband to call in sick and stay home with me. Back then, I was afraid, not a problem now.

Then one morning, an overnight guest came down for breakfast and told me about the unbelievably creepy thing that had happened to him during the night. While lying in bed, he was treated to a rear view of a big black dog walking around his bed. At first, he thought it was our dog, our beloved dark gray old English Sheepdog. The thing of it was, though, how had he gotten through that closed door? But it did indeed, and then the next thing our guest knew was that this thing, this almost-dog thing, was on his bed and paw imprints started making their way up the blanket towards his head. Paralyzed by fear, he just lay there, waiting to see what was going to happen next. Once it reached him, however, it disappeared into thin air. After hearing about this I was now sure—as sure as I needed to be—that we had something in our home; something that was evil. I believe in my heart our guest might have just seen a HELL HOUND, like the kind you hear about, the kind you might read about in books or see in movies.

But to think this thing could be real! OMG.

During the next several months I would see huge insects, black in color, half a dozen at a time, resembling grasshoppers and ranging from around one to two feet long, walking up the walls and across the ceiling of our bedroom. You would think I was on some kind of an LSD trip, but I hadn't taken anything! I tended to believe it was my imagination, a reflection, or my eyes playing tricks on me. The one thing I NEVER thought—or at least never dared to think—was that I was actually, really seeing them.

We started hearing knocks on our bedroom doors and even on our bed posts. Heading to a room and having the door slam right in our face just before we entered fast became a familiar experience. This was so bad that our housekeepers who had been with us for over three years, suddenly quit. In her phone message, she said that we needed our home blessed because there was something really bad in it!

Finally, after all the shock and horror, the climax came in the form of the shadow man standing right over me one night until I bolted upright from a prone position and caused him to take two steps back and vanish.

It was at this point I realized it had been only 15 inches or so from my face. As it stood there looking down on me, I had the opportunity to get a good look at it. It stood over six-foot-tall, solid, slender and Spiderman-like and had the longest arms and fingers I had ever seen. And to make this strange creature look even worse, it was holding its arms straight down, directly by its side flexing its long creepy fingers.

I was horror-struck! The panic that overcame me literally took my breath away and paralyzed my entire body. It took a few moments for me to gain my composure. I immediately took a deep breath so I would not black out with this creature standing directly in front of me. It just stood there looking straight at me. I then let out a scream that was sufficiently horrifying to jolt my soundly sleeping husband into a sitting position with a look of astonishment on his face that I will never, ever forget.

The Spiderman immediately vanished, disappearing in a flash. I could barely get the words out of my mouth to describe to my husband what had just occurred. WTH was that? I had never seen anything like that before! I believed I had just seen my first demon.

We had gone years and years with no unpleasant surprises in that house and all of a sudden something so creepy and unbelievable comes out of nowhere!

I could never get over what had happened. I could never feel safe there again. I could never be alone in the house. And the biggest thing was I could NEVER sleep in the dark again to this day. Since then, a light is always burning on my nightstand. So, eventually we sold our home and moved far away, never to return.

OUR BATTLE WITH SATAN'S SIDEKICK

What caused the energy in this house to suddenly change after three years of peace and tranquility? Well, that was the light bulb moment. Sidekick had stayed with us on several occasions. I never connected the dots until the week I helped move my sister into her daughter's home.

KAREN'S STORY

We had been residing in Las Vegas two years when the following incident occurred.

Early one morning, after Oscar had left for work, I was in bed listening to the sound of quiet in our room, enjoying the moment before the busy day started. All of a sudden, I hear this hefty sound radiating from the back bedroom, down the hall. The noise morphed into footsteps, however not human footsteps. In my terrified, alert state my brain was screaming at me, "Those footsteps are hooves!" As the alarming clamor of hooves slowly progressed down the long hall to the entrance of my bedroom, my fear level was rising off the charts!

Before I even saw it, I felt the horrific energy of whatever it was. As I gradually slid further underneath my bedding, never taking my eyes off the doorway, the "thing" came to a halt. What the hell was it!? My first instinct was to cry out for help, but when I began to scream, the only sound that escaped my throat was a low, pathetic squawk. The sight of it immediately made me stop breathing; I was holding my breath, dreading what it would do next!

The only way to describe this "thing" was a goat demon! At this time in my life, I was a goat demon virgin, so what did I know? Nothing! The thoughts were flying around my head so fast I was getting dizzy! Or was the dizziness and nausea from the demon itself? Omg, it moved into the center of my bedroom!

Then it extended/opened huge 15 ft wings on either side of its body. Since setting its sights on me, its round, red eyes never left my face. I took a deep breath, jumped out of bed, fell on my knees and prayed like my life depended on it because I was pretty sure it did! As soon as I cried out, "Jesus," it vanished; however, the evil energy hung in the air for another 10 minutes.

The back room was where Sidekick always stayed when he visited us. He had only left a week before this "thing" manifested. Do I need to say more? I was clueless of this connection at the time.

That's when I began to see the giant spiders crawling up my walls and onto the ceiling. I thought it was just the ravings of an insomniac (me), however there was more to it than that.

When we left Brentwood, my husband was working on a pretty extensive job, he was still working on it our first two years in Las Vegas. The story is a sizable one, but I'm going to make it short and fast.

The job went bad, we lost our entire savings plus some, then 2008 hit before we could recoup. We lost our beautiful home. One day my sister and I were discussing what had happened when my dead mother screamed, "Belcastro!!"

At first, I was stunned, slowly settling into my "Lightbulb Moment." My husband had his own business for 21 years and had not once made a poor estimate on a project or taken a bad job. My dead mother said it was Sidekick's revenge for taking my daughter away from him when we moved a state away.

Then I thought about the truly gorgeous home we had in California. That picture-perfect house and award-winning back yard sold four times in a two-year period! It's really unbelievable!

Sidekick practically lived at that house! Again, do I need to say more?

DEMON BLOCK

Brand new printer and I can't get it to work! I have been printing to the upstairs printer and I'm having to go up there to get print outs when everyone knows I don't go upstairs for anything (demons and bad knee)! My husband came home, and the printer works, going through the exact same process as me! Again, I look crazy and incompetent. Interestingly enough, my printer does not work for my daughter either. Only my husband.

II

I Am Back
and Stronger
✝

Karen Pena

When I returned from my sister's a few days before Christmas, I was healthier. Thanks to my daily smoothie, my ulcers were vanishing rapidly, and I was feeling stronger by the day. The biggest improvement, though, took place surrounding my mental health. I put the extra helping of down time which I enjoyed during that period to good use by evaluating my experiences with/in other dimensions over the previous nine months. I looked at what went wrong and what had gone right (if anything), and after mentally revisiting that very dark space, I believed that there was only one acceptable plan of attack for me if I was to survive for any length of time in that house. Since I was without physical emotional support in Hell's sublet, it was obvious that I would have to rely solely on myself to get the job done right.

The first thing I did was to consciously close down. In fact, I shut down completely—and it worked. My entire attitude changed for the better, and instead of seeing demons every day and night, I saw only one or two a week. Even with this fortuitous turn of events, though, there were still some weird things occurring. One of them had to do with the hellhound that appeared almost every day. What might have made my blood chill the first time around, though, hit me completely differently this time. Actually, it made me laugh, by virtue of the fact that he showed up only when there was food involved. I knew the demons were still there, and I didn't care, since I no longer let their negative energy or demonic voices freak me out.

The second thing I did was take back the power from my daughter where Sidekick was concerned. I had my own voice now, and I would use it rather than let my daughter handle—or rather mishandle—the situation. I was older and wiser than her. Besides, I'd felt all along that letting her have total control was a big mistake. I was finally ready to deal with Sidekick but in an entirely dissimilar way than before. What had changed for me was . . . me! It had to do with the way I felt deep in my soul, and I don't think it would be an exaggeration to say that I had gone through a radical transformation. I no longer saw myself as a victim or felt like one, which brings me to the third change I made.

I asked myself, "What does an abused, broken and mentally challenged Satan worshiper really need?" I decided that what he needed most was kindness. I was determined to put aside my anger towards Sidekick after promising God that I would attempt to treat Sidekick with the same kindness, love and thoughtfulness that Jesus exhibited throughout the New Testament. As lofty as this goal was, it was, nevertheless, full speed ahead for my new course of action. I started to work on changing my attitude towards him, showing him so much kindness and love that he didn't know what hit him. He began to change, becoming noticeably calmer and at times even coming out with a demon-free laugh or two. The tension in the house decreased considerably! The timing of this transformation couldn't have been more fortunate. It was, in a way, a case of "out of the frying pan and into the fire," while we watched life outside the house and everywhere in the world change drastically as Covid-19 turned the world upside down.

It all happened so fast. My husband, considered to be an essential worker, continued to go to work every day. My daughter, on the other hand, was able to work from home, and OMG, having her home every day made everything much, much better! Sidekick was on his best behavior and I finally had some help in handling him. As difficult as "lockdown" was, it was at the same time strangely comfortable in some weird way. My sister and I decided that this intense and exciting time was the perfect opportunity for us to complete our first book *The Hauntings of Two Sisters— Shocking True Life Experiences.* I grew to love the daily walks in the desert that I'd started to take and welcomed a new puppy into our lives. My new Keto diet was doing a wonderful job of controlling my diabetes, and with all these changes for the better, I was at peace for the first time since moving in with my daughter.

One thing that Sidekick and I had in common was our love of cooking. Since eating out was one of the pandemic's first casualties, I decided that I would dive deep into my cooking skills and make us all happy with some dishes to remember (false modesty aside, I have to say that this girl can cook)! Truth be told, I earned my stripes the hard way in the kitchen. Okay, this is hilarious. The first Thanksgiving dinner I ever cooked as a married woman couldn't have been a bigger disaster. I left the neck and innards inside the turkey, and then proceeded to burn it until it was so dry that not one person in that house of guests could chew it! Seriously humbled by this episode, I spent the next 30 years taking cooking classes and teaching myself to cook whatever I desired. For our first lockdown feast I went way back to my mom's and grandmother's recipes and the dishes I had adored growing up. I didn't stop there, inviting my husband to make a happy trip down memory lane by whipping up a few of his mother's favorite meals.

It's really very simple. Cooking brings me incredible joy.

Sidekick's specialty is stew and soup, and when experimenting with new dishes he's a total perfectionist. I bought him spices to his heart's content and just about anything else he needed to create his masterpieces, including a notebook in which he could record the recipes for his creations. My daughter's cooking skills and desire to know her way around a kitchen being nonexistent, it was really enjoyable to have someone to collaborate with in the kitchen. The result was equally enjoyable, a nightly procession of elaborate, over the top dinners with wines to match. It brought back memories of earlier experiences with fine dining, one of which was my long-ago membership in the old Supper Club.

All told, I had three solid months of tranquility: March, April and May of 2020.

Sidekick had never experienced a family dinner (what the hell), and I was counting on our collaboration in the kitchen and the great dinners that followed to help undo some of the damage he had suffered growing up. I just couldn't, however, ignore the signs that were beginning to point in the opposite direction. As much as I wanted to believe that the kindness and love were having their effect on him, it was apparent that his mental instability was beginning to work its way up to the surface again. The meltdowns started off small and happened infrequently. Then it happened. One day I was in the garage smoking and talking on the phone with my sister, when Sidekick approached me and asked if we could talk. I'm thinking to myself, "Shit!" Emotional roller coaster that he is, I had no idea where this particular ride was going to take me. Nevertheless, I put a big smile on my face and fired back with a "Yes, of course!" I repeatedly told myself, "Think of Jesus, think of Jesus!"

The conversation opener was nothing if not blunt. Sidekick looked me straight in the eye and said, "What's wrong with me?" Having been on the receiving end of more than a few clever, if diabolical, ploys on his part, my reaction to this new tack on his part was guarded. After all, it could easily have been a trick question. After silently deliberating whether I should fire back with, "Let's start with a reality check; you worship Satan," I decided on a less confrontational course of action that involved saying nothing while I just let him talk. And he did talk; so much, in fact, that four and a half hours along and a pack of cigarettes later, we were both emotionally exhausted and done for the day.

I have to admit, I was completely caught off guard by what he said. He poured his heart out, something which, irony of ironies, very well might not have happened if he wasn't high on something. In any case, it was too much for me, and when he broke down crying and sobbing, my heart went out to him. At that moment, my memories of all the horrific things he had done to me ceased to exist and were replaced by a determination to do whatever I could to help heal the emotional pain of this deeply troubled soul.

I gently ministered to him, assuring him that God's infinite love was his for the taking whether he believed he was worthy of it or not. I kept on emphasizing the fact that God would and could take that pain away, and that all he had to do to make this happen was to just let Him in. As it turned out, I was running into more than a bit of interference while laying this information on this poor, suffering man. Every single time I mentioned God, my dead father would scream, "No Karen!" in my ear. I chose to ignore this bit of advice and carried on—despite having learned from past experience with departed love ones that when they came to you with advice from beyond the grave it behooves you to listen. After confessing that he had hurt, tortured and taken revenge on a good number of people, Sidekick tried to whitewash his actions by assuring me that they all stemmed from his strong sense of justice. These people had done terrible things and they needed to die. When he started to actually name names and share some gruesome details, I began to lose it! OMG, wouldn't you? In all my 61 years, I had never dealt with anything remotely like this. Although I was definitely in way over my head,

I kept it to myself, letting no sign of my inner turmoil show in my facial expression nor in my demeanor.

So, he went on, insisting repeatedly that even though he desperately wanted to be a good person, there was no fixing him. The sobs came in an unending barrage, punctuated every so often by, "What's wrong with me? What's wrong with me?" Again, I just continued to quietly minister to him while the tears rolled down my face, assuring him of the positive consequences of allowing Jesus into his heart. My ability to counsel him came from the strength that had come to me by the grace of God when I forgave Sidekick. I let him know point blank that when I look at him, I see a man in overwhelming emotional pain, and he let me know in return that he was well aware of my insight into his condition.

With my dad still screaming in my ears, I thought of all the people I'd ministered to over the years and of how this particular ministry was the most important I'd ever been involved in. My prayer was gut-deep and to the point: "God give me the words and wisdom I need to deal with this broken man."

Regarding my father's screaming, I understood why he had to do it. He knew that the demons would come after me full force because of my Godly session with Sidekick. Demons or no demons, however, quitting just wasn't an option for me. One thing a Christian can't allow herself to be is a coward, and the well-known call for personal courage from *(Psalms 23:4 "Even though I walk through the darkest valley, I will fear no evil, for you are with me; your rod and your staff, they comfort me.")* were not just words we repeat at church every Sunday. Again, Christians can't be cowards. No matter then, that this man had tortured me for over a year now; I was fully prepared to put my hands on him and pray, with his help, for Jesus to come into his heart.

Sadly, though, as much as I yearned for a positive outcome for this tortured soul, it just wasn't going to happen. The decision, in the end, was his to make, and the decision he finally made was to continue on a path that could lead only to self-destruction. Even though the sum total of my history with this man was not a good one— again, if not for my dead mother and my sister, I would have lost my life—I ended my conversation with him on a kind and gentle note. After reminding him that God and I loved him, I walked into my bedroom and broke down sobbing. I was so utterly drained by this whole thing that all I could think of doing was to ask God how a soul could be so twisted and warped and in such emotional pain. It hit me at that moment that as badly shattered as Sidekick's soul was (extreme trauma can do this), God could still repair it. It was all so incredibly frustrating. I made sure that I was prayed up for that night, fully accepting a powerful demon attack that, thanks to God, never came. The Lord was in full protection mode, as I found out later that night when I walked into the living room to find a dozen angels standing shoulder to shoulder with arms entwined.

For days afterward, Sidekick would not look at me nor have anything to do with me. I understood; he had shared things with me that he had probably never shared with anyone. I was grateful for the temporary period of peace, a period which, unfortunately, did not last long. I began to get sick again. Things became worse all too quickly, with his meltdowns and anger again out of control.

Round two, here we go!

DEMON BLOCK

Pam sat down to write at her desk along with her dog, Dexter. All of a sudden her 80-pound Goldendoodle began to act as if he was fighting something that was hitting his body underneath her desk. This went on for five minutes. After it was over, her dog had a hard time getting up or even walking. She and her husband took him immediately to the animal ER. After four long hours of anxiously waiting, all the test results came back negative. Her dog was not normal again for three days.

12

Can you Hear
Me Now
✝

Pam Mandel

Months and months went by and things still hadn't changed.

Good old Sidekick was as fast on his feet as ever in the dirty tricks department. He had the advantage of knowing our plans well in advance, and this allowed him to consistently stay one step ahead of us. The evidence for this was everywhere and overwhelming. In fact, so much so, that we hardly knew where to begin trying to figure out how he was able to get the drop on us every time! While my sister held firm in her conviction that his minions functioned as his willing and able spy network (some of his knowledge was that), I begged to differ. Being no stranger to the unusual world of communication with the other side, I knew full well just how vague the ghost's line of communication can be. Could it be different with the communication of fallen angels (demons)? Or could this be something else entirely? So, I placed my proverbial chips elsewhere regarding Sidekick's information source(s). I had a strong hunch it wouldn't go away, and that hunch had something to do with some kind of electronic listening device.

One morning, while Karen was relaxing in the backyard, her daughter came out to let her know that Sidekick was absolutely infuriated by what he'd overheard us saying about him. This was a charge to which we would have to plead guilty. From a practical point of view, though, there was something extremely puzzling about this. How did he manage to hear us? My sister and I got on the phone and began to seriously try to brainstorm our way to an answer. We concluded that since his room was directly above my sister's, there was a very good chance that he was listening through a vent. In response, we got into the habit of whispering as quietly as we could when Karen was in her room or, better yet not even bothering to converse unless we were outside, in the backyard or in her car.

Shortly thereafter, something happened that allowed us to discover the pack of demons that were attached to Sidekick. A friend of ours named Aileen added his name to the list of beneficiaries of daily prayer that she had inscribed in her Bible. Several months later, when we discovered that he was performing nightly rituals, we relayed our findings to Aileen, who immediately burned the piece of paper that had his name on it. I was telling my sister the next morning about it on the phone. I immediately shared the news of Aileen's reaction with my sister. A few hours later, when she was in the kitchen helping herself to a cup of coffee, she was suddenly confronted by a very upset Sidekick who, after demanding to know, "Who the hell is Aileen?" stormed off ranting and raving about her.

Woooo!!!???? How did he know? So, the mystery continues.

One day Sidekick said that he was going out for several hours. Seeing an opportunity to strike back, Karen procured a bundle of sage and some holy water for a total cleanse of the house. With both of us on the phone together, we got right to the business at hand. We prayed together fervently as my sister started to sweep the entire house with our spiritual weapons. Suddenly, with barely a small portion of the house done, Sidekick came bursting through the front door screaming at her at the top of his lungs, "I know what you've been up to. I know what you have been doing. I am going to tell your husband what you are doing." It seems that Mr. S, however, was in for a rude awakening. My sister was in this one to win it, and instead of being cowed by yet another all-out frontal assault by Mr. Big Bad Bully, she fired back with, "Don't you dare come up on me like that. Why don't you just chill and do another ritual or whatever you do." He took a step back, shocked into momentary paralysis by the verbal one-two she'd just handed him. His dark eyes got even darker—darker and so big that it looked like their sockets might not be able to hold them much longer. But my sister wasn't done yet, and countered his feeble attempt at a counterpunch with a mean verbal uppercut, "What? You don't think I know things too?" He stormed towards the front door, threatening to tell her husband all about the cleansing. Even threatening to disclose a few dirty little secrets about his daughter. As he marched outside and headed to the spot where her husband was working, my sister called after him, "Go for it and see just how well telling Jennifer's dad horrible things about her works out for you."

My sister said the look on his face confirmed everything we'd surmised. It was a look of pure shock and disbelief at our having cracked the code, figuring out his huge secret. She might have done a victory dance right then and there if it weren't for one little thing. This was hardly the first time she had seen his anger and hate. After all, it's pretty much where he lives. The anger and hate she could hear in his voice this time, though, well fearsome just might be an understatement.

But life went on—as it always does—in the house that had become the sublet from Hell. One day my sister and I got to talking about the messages we had received over the years from our mom. Regarding things psychic, our boy was still on a roll. For later in the day, while my sister was preparing something in the kitchen, Sidekick ran downstairs, sat on the couch with his head in his hands and said, "Why won't your dead mother shut the fxxx up?"

In the living room, Karen was having a discussion with her daughter concerning Sidekick's lack of effort and help around the house. Jennifer agreed. An hour later, Sidekick begins a manic two hours of intense cleaning. A coincidence? I think not. Hmm, this could work in our favor.

But again, how did he know?

A few weeks later in the garage (see chapter 6), Aileen, Karen and I were searching furiously for the jewelry that he'd stolen from my sister. Once again, he knew exactly what we were up to. How? What on earth was going on here? One morning my niece, appearing to be extremely pissed off about something, joined Karen in her bedroom for a mutual venting session about Sidekick's cleanliness. Whispering to prevent him from overhearing the conversation, the two of them agreed that they were fed up with Sidekick's leaving a mess in the kitchen every time he used it. Seriously, the guy cooked half a pound of bacon a morning! And again, it was Psychic City, here we come, as within the hour he came downstairs to announce to one and all that he was going to give the kitchen a good cleaning! WTH? At least we're getting something positive out of all this. My sister went in her room and had a good laugh.

In the months that followed, incidents of this kind, happened one after the other, with Sidekick having foreknowledge of upcoming events. My sister was convinced that his minions were giving him complete transcripts of the conversations we'd been having in the house. For lack of hard proof to the contrary, I agreed to her suggestion about doing our talking in the backyard or in someone's car. Please understand. It's not that I was convinced that Karen was right. Even though I'd had way too much experience with the supernatural to think that life was as predictable as math, I still felt that there had to be a more logical explanation for what was going on. So, I did some online research on listening devices. After looking at a variety of models, shapes and sizes, we ended up going for a wireless bug detector that emits a signal that is capable of discovering any bugs that were in the area. There was, by the way, some evidence of a non-technological nature that supported my belief that we were giving the minions much too much credit for spying on us. Sidekick's highly detailed knowledge of the content of our conversations just didn't jive with our experience of communicating with other dimensions. The messages we'd received from them had typically been on the vague side. Ergo, by process of elimination, the most obvious explanation for Sidekick's apparent omniscience was that he was using a listening device or many listening devices. Perhaps one in every location.

Fast forward a bit. Karen is sitting on her bed one morning. The TV is off; there is complete silence in the room. She hears the sound of a switch being flipped and a burst of static coming from a spot close to her nightstand. Eureka!

Our suspicions were confirmed. We both breathed that proverbial sigh of relief that comes when you finally find out that you have cracked the mystery. Since our device still hadn't arrived, we decided to use whatever weapon(s) were at our disposal for the time being. In this case, it involved finding a way to use his listening devices to our advantage. Basically, Karen got the entire house cleaned, laughing out loud, because Sidekick wasn't aware of our knowledge at the time.

Our dead mom confirmed there were listening devices, and not just one but several.

And so, the next phase of Operation Catch Sidekick began.

Karen and I started timing our morning talks to begin as soon as she heard the above-mentioned static-y sound. After she put me on speaker, we would talk about this book—the one you're reading right now—and focus on deciding which chapters to include. During one of our discussions, I started off with "Sidekick, can you hear us now?"

Direct hit!! My sister could tell by his attitude later in the day that there was no doubt that he was indeed electronically eavesdropping on us. His anger quickly ratcheted up; he had no choice but to keep his knowledge to himself. I mean really, was the poor fool going to confess that he had placed listening devices all throughout the house, and even in our vehicles? Yes, we also had good reason to believe that they'd been placed in both my sister's and her daughter's vehicles. Karen and I soon learned to look for a simple pattern that was based on noticing how the content of our morning telephone calls affected his mood and attitude later in the day.

Finally, the Wireless Bug Detector Signal device arrived, and we got to work rooting out every single "bug" that he'd planted on us.

Closely following the directions that came with the device, we started with my sister's bedroom (talk about the lack of boundaries). There were two spots where the device went full-on loco: the closet and the nightstand. So far so good, except for the little technical obstacle we'd run into while using our bug detector. Ordinarily, we'd just ask my sister's husband to lend his considerable technical expertise to help us clear up the problem. Ordinarily, he would have been glad to oblige. Unfortunately, this situation just didn't qualify as "ordinary" with him. Why? It was simple. He thought we were bat shit crazy and wanted nothing to do with this whole cat-and-mouse game we were playing with Sidekick. Nevertheless, my sister and I continued with our campaign.

Around the time when my sister took refuge from the rapidly deteriorating situation with Sidekick, showing up at my house suitcase in hand, I was hard at work trying to detect any listening devices that might be in her car. After scoring a direct hit right away, the detector went crazy when I held it up against the speakers that were embedded in the side doors. I quietly continued with my hunt before Sidekick figured out what I was up to.

The upside—and I won't underestimate how badly we needed some good news at that point—is that at last, I was in firm possession of the trump card in this little game of cat-and-mouse we were playing. I was miles away and there was nothing he could do to stop me! Things were becoming more and more interesting, and I decided to kick back a bit and have some fun. Knowing that he was listening in, I began to up the ante. When the device went silent it was because, fearing he'd been digitally busted, he had turned it off. Without fail, though, his curiosity would get the best of him. He would turn it back on a few minutes later. When that happened, I would just hold my device up to where I thought he had planted a bug. If it went from silent to crazy, I would simply say "Can you hear me now?" After about four rounds of this he would throw in the towel and turn everything off for the night. This behavior was dangerous. Pissing him off always was.

Yay!!!!! Finally!!!!

The next morning, it seemed like a good idea to verify the locations of the bugs Sidekick had planted. We just wanted to double check the vehicle before we took it to an upholstery service to have the door panels removed and photographs taken of the devices that had been planted. By that time, Karen and I were not at all bothered by the opinions of others as to our sanity or lack of same. We were finally on a roll and we were looking forward to getting the proof that we so desperately needed. When I checked things out at six in the morning, there was no activity on my signal detector. By 9:00 am it began to go crazy, so I verified each and every location where he'd placed a listening device. Happy that we were on the cusp of solving this problem, I even said a hearty "good morning" to our nemesis Mr. S on our way out the door! We took the car to an upholstery service, as planned, and watched while they took the door panels off.

No deal!

Not a single device was found. Now, doubting ourselves, we were thinking maybe we were crazy. Over nineteen months of no one believing us and my sister's husband waving off our suspicions with, "You were just talking too loud." We knew otherwise. But then it happened. My sister got a text from her daughter Jennifer: "Are you, Michael, and Pam going to be home today between 1:00 pm and 3:00 pm?" To which Karen replied, "Yes, but why?" Jennifer responded with, "I will tell you later." At 1:45 pm Michael got a call on his cellphone that came with a "Restricted" warning. When he answered his phone, it turned out to be Jennifer wanting to speak to Karen.

Okay, that was weird. Karen's daughter then told her that she was sure that her cell phone had been compromised. In other words, someone (Sidekick) was listening to her calls. She then told Karen that in the future, she will use her new burner phone to call her and that her calls will be made to my husband's phone. Remember, we have been telling Jennifer for months that we were being listened to. She really thought we were crazy and had lost it.

Having finally gotten some real evidence, she was beginning to believe us. Two days later, after we'd spent months trying to convince him that we were being listened to as well, my sister's husband filed a similar report. As good as it felt to finally have the rest of the family on board with my sister and me, we had to hold off on doing a happy dance. Because at this point, communicating over the 600 miles that separated us became a lot more complicated. No one knew exactly how sophisticated Sidekick's electronic eavesdropping campaign was. So, we thought it best to limit our communication to a call placed every few days by Jennifer to my husband's cell phone. We also placed a moratorium on discussing the matter in the house. But instead, holding our conversations about Operation Catch Sidekick outside, away from house or even in the middle of the friggin´ desert!

And then it happened again!

I know that I have written the above with tongue in cheek humor but let me be serious for a moment. His listening devices put us at such a disadvantage! Sidekick was performing his nightly rituals based on what we were discussing daily. It put my sister and me in terrible danger, and even our dead mother was kicked out of the house. The thought of anyone using a listening device was completely alien to us. Who would have thought? Is this a typical M.O. for Satan worshipers?

One night, Karen's husband was sitting in the living room watching TV when Sidekick came downstairs and asked if he could show him something. He disappeared into the garage and brought a big ladder into the house, which he then placed under the smoke detector. He climbed up to where the smoke detector was, opened it up, and removed a small device. After showing it to

Karen's husband, he informed him that this was the listening device that we had been talking about and he knew everything we had said about him. With this surprising turn of events, it looked like we had found the bit of validation for which we'd been desperately looking. But wait! Did Sidekick actually think that by showing us a single listening device that he was going to convince us that there was only one?

No way. We knew there were more of them planted throughout the house, in our vehicles, and who knows where else? We were right. There were several other devices in the house, and as for our failure to find his electronic bugs in our cars, there was a simple explanation—he'd hacked into our Bluetooth system!

Hurray!!!!

We were not crazy after all!

PHOTO GALLERY

Karen and Pam

Our Grandparents With Us

Our Parents With Us

Pam and Karen

JUNE 19-23, 2020

The trip was on!

My sister, her husband and daughter were going to join Michael and me at Big Bear in Southern California for a long weekend of summer fun in the fresh mountain air.

Since our families each had two doggies and needed to book a pair of not-too-plentiful dog-friendly cabins, we played it safe and made our reservations over a month in advance. Our cabins were about a mile away from each other, a situation which worked out well. Michael and I planned on coming in Friday and leaving on Tuesday morning. My niece's attempt to move the first night of her stay one night up from Saturday to Friday didn't quite work out perfectly; the upshot being that she had to reserve a different cabin just for Friday night. Moving twice in 24 hours was a bit of a hassle, of course, but I guess it was worth it to them to begin their vacation early.

Sidekick (thank God) was not planning on joining us since he was going to be out of town working with his Dad for two weeks. Needless to say, at this point (see previous chapters in this book), my sister and I were not at all unhappy about him being gone those few weeks. Once our vacation was over, in fact, we had plans to give their house and her daughter a good spiritual cleansing. Saving her, hopefully, from the Demonic Fog and removing any spells that he might have cast over her with his sick rituals. Also clearing her mind so that she might be able to see just what an evil man he truly was. This would be our chance to finally get some blessed relief from the awful chaos the demons were bringing down on all our heads.

Although we had planned on taking our pickup so that we could fit all our gear comfortably, two weeks before our trip the truck started having problems. At first, one of the windows refused to open and shut, soon to be joined by a sunroof that behaved likewise. Two different motors had to be ordered, and since the vehicle was not going to be ready by our trip date, we ended up taking my Cadillac. There were two problems with this. First of all, without the ample cargo space offered by the pickup truck, we had to leave some of the items home. Also, the Cadillac rides low—not the best state of affairs for navigating the mountain roads and tough terrain that we encountered.

Michael and I arrived before my sister and her family did, so right after we checked into our cabin, we ventured out to purchase groceries for our stay. The cabin was nice, with a really large deck that the dogs just couldn't get enough of and two large TVs inside. Despite being a bit short on extras, everything looked clean and neat. Since Karen's most recent update informed us that they were only an hour away, Michael and I went to get dinner so we could all dine in their cabin for the one night they had booked there. The place gave off a warm feeling. It also came with a few of those touches that can make you feel so special: lotions, soaps, coffees, flavored creams, etc. What's more, all the towels were folded perfectly! We all enjoyed dinner and a good round of catch-up conversation. After our long drive through the mountains, Michael and I decided to retire early. The weekend's full line up of activities was going to kick off first thing in the morning with some wave runner action!

Their check out time was 11:00 am, and the cabin they were moving into had a check in time of 4:00 pm. Accordingly, we based the next day's activities on their moving schedule. Much of the afternoon was spent hanging out in our cabin. By the time they left shortly before four, we'd made arrangements to meet them at their new digs for dinner at around 6:00 pm. As was the case with so many things in the preceding months, COVID-19 had the last word on what we could do and what we couldn't do. Since the dine-in option wasn't available because of the virus, restaurants were only doing take-out orders. We were hungry, so we wasted no time in sitting down at the computer and placing our dinner order online. Unfortunately, our cabin was not within their delivery area, so we had to head over to the restaurant to pick up our order.

This all took time and finally, our take-out was ready. Famished by this point, my sister and I double-timed our way towards the kitchen table while everyone else remained on the beautiful large deck with comfy chairs and a lakeview.

Then it happened.

I opened the front door and after taking five or so steps into the cabin, I could no longer move. There was something evil there; something so overwhelming, so strong, so terrifying that greeted me right at the door. OMG, what is this? My sister's first cabin and our cabin were so pleasant; why not this one? I decided to take a deep breath and head for the kitchen table so I could sit down. What a mistake that was. This feeling was swallowing me whole at this point, the feeling that I was the sole focus of whatever it was that was zapping me with that stinking energy! I sat down at the kitchen table, stunned into silence by the

creepy energy that had overtaken me. I tried to get a reading on what had just invaded my inner space. It got worse.
After the first bite of my salad I was so nauseous that I
could hardly look at my food. My sister sat down next to
me and immediately picked up on the fact that something
was very, very wrong. I knew she had to sleep there for the
next two nights, so when she asked me if I was okay, I de-
bated whether to tell her exactly what I was feeling.

All of a sudden something banged so hard against my
right hip that it jolted my entire body. That's when I told
her, whispering so soft that no one else could hear, that
there's something very evil in this cabin. Something so evil
that I have only felt what I was feeling just then one other
time in my entire life. I began to feel really sick, so sick
that I knew if I didn't leave right then this thing was going
to take serious action against me! I told her in no uncertain terms that I had to go and had to go that instant.
Incredibly, she felt none of the energy that I was feeling!

Uninhibited demonic intimidation plus ghoulish physical contact was more than I bargained for on this vacation
(as a reminder, #2 on our Top Ten List). So, I got my salad
and my purse and headed straight for the front door.
Whatever it was decided to keep me company on my way
out, literally breathing down my neck as I walked through
the doorway and outside to the deck to join everyone else.
My husband who had just started eating was shocked when
I told him we had to go. As we walked past my sister's husband, the Ghost Denying Skeptic, he jumped up and, with
his arms crossed over his chest, said, "I have the worst chill

all of a sudden." I wanted to say, "Duh. Can you see who is walking behind me Mr. Skeptic?"

I made my way over to the stairs. Using both hands, I steadied myself as well as I could by gripping the handrail and slowly descended the 12 extremely steep steps. I was just waiting for whatever it was to push me down those stairs. After that final step I made a beeline for the car and, as we were leaving, I let my sister know I would not be coming back there again. So, for the duration of our stay, family socializing would have to be done at our cabin. Once we were in the car, my husband noticed the look on my face. It was then he got over the initial shock of our leaving before he had had a chance to eat his dinner. He knew something was really wrong. I guess that's why he decided to lay off with the questions.

Finally, we arrived safely at our evil-free home away from home where I was simply delighted to have felt no presence of evil. As exhausted as I was from what I'd just experienced, I still felt it would be a good idea to fill Michael in on what had happened to me at my sister's cabin. At least, that's what I thought. After I shared my awful experiences of that evening with him, we both turned in for the night. It was really hot in our un-air-conditioned cabin, so I slept on top of the covers. About an hour after finally falling asleep, I was abruptly awakened by the strangest sensation. I felt the sheet underneath me moving on its own toward the edge of the bed. I knew it had nothing to do with my husband since he wasn't moving at all. Also, the sheet was moving in the wrong direction for its movement to be due to anything on his part. By the time the sheet was down two feet, I felt one of the most unnerving feelings I'd ever known. I was in total shock and disbelief. An alarm went off in my brain. WTH was this!

And then I knew.

It was the evil entity letting me know that he'd found me. He knew exactly where I was. To say the least, the rest of the night was spent on edge. The next day we had rented a boat and raft for the lake. We finished it off with a wonderful time in the quaint little town of Big Bear. During our time there, I contacted a demonologist to see if he could help us cleanse the house while Sidekick was away. After a few back and forth emails with him on the situation, he encouraged me to lose his phone number and never, ever again mention his name or what we were planning on doing. I could feel his fear long distance. Again, I did not understand why a "demonologist," of all people, would be so afraid. They were supposed to be the people that were the least afraid of these situations! It was sort of an oxymoron!

The next day we all headed home.

When we got back, my sister and I resumed working on our plan for preparing the cleansing of both the house and her daughter, who suddenly laid some very distressing news on us. Sidekick was cutting his trip short by over a week and was due to arrive the next day.

Interesting timing on the evil boy's part . . . did he know what we were planning? If so, how could he know?

After getting home, I started to reflect on what had

happened to me. Why was the demon only at the second cabin my sister stayed at but not the first cabin they stayed in nor at our cabin? The answer came to me immediately. Sidekick only had the address of my sisters second cabin, since that was the cabin they'd booked originally. He did not know our cabin's location and, since their first cabin was last minute, he didn't have that one either.

We could only conclude, after deliberation, that Sidekick had dispatched the demon to focus on me and me alone. Maybe it was because he heard me through his listening devices say, "If Sidekick is going, then I'm not!"

Pam and Karen

I desperately needed to write a chapter about this particular demon because of the influence he had exerted over me from the get-go. I introduced him in the chapter entitled "Nightly Tortures":

Of all the stories I can share, at this point, I want to share what I call the smoking demon story. At that time in my life, I was a smoker and, again, I am walking the house all through the night unable to sleep. Around 2:00 am I went into the backyard to have a cigarette. I was sleep deprived and honestly, an emotional mess. I sat down in my smoking chair, lit my cigarette, took a few puffs when all of a sudden, this horrific looking demon bent right over me with his face an inch from mine! Surprisingly, this particular demon actually had a face. He had four-inch horns at the front of his head, one on each side, squinty eyes but his mouth was opened, full of pointed jagged teeth as if something had filed them sharp. No sooner had the sight of those gruesome horns and teeth taken my consciousness hostage, when a very distasteful thought came to me. Was this extremely unappealing creature actually smiling at me? Standing next to him was a four-legged representative of the Nether Regions, a hellhound whose breed I immediately recognized. He was a grey Italian Cane Corso, a truly beautiful dog despite where he came from. He was so big that his back was almost level with the demon's waist.

Then, exhausted from a lack of sleep, I was graced with a formidable courage that sometimes comes to those who are just too tired to care. Blowing a stream of smoke right in its hideous face, I then proceeded to tell him off in no uncertain terms. I believe my exact words were "You evil piece of shit! How dare you try to intimidate me like this! You chose the wrong side and you don't even have your wings anymore! How's your undying reverence to your master Satan working out for you?!" Speech delivered, I put my cigarette out and went back in the house. Well this was not the smartest move. From then on, the house's designated ghoul pack always accompanied me when I went out into the back yard for a smoke.

I'm not a person who smokes because they crave nicotine or because it's a daily habit that's been with me so long it's hard to break. Although I think both of these factors have had some authority over me, they still don't tell the whole story. The fact of the matter is that like my father, I have always enjoyed smoking. For what it's worth, I have never stayed a smoker for long periods of time, maybe a year here and there. This time, unfortunately, I went back to smoking when I turned 50. It was especially crazy, since it had already been over 10 years—my longest smoke-free stretch yet— since I had last lit up. My mother (dead or alive) absolutely detested my smoking habit. Even after her passing, many of the messages I received from her were impassioned requests for me to quit immediately. I would never dismiss a message from Mom, especially if they were as urgent as those I just mentioned. But I hadn't yet—and maybe couldn't—even begun to anticipate the effect the Smoking Demon would have on me. "Play Mind Games" (#8 on our Top Ten List)

The honest truth is that after the above-mentioned business with this ghoulish creature, anywhere or anytime I paused to have a cigarette, or even just craved one—be it in Las Vegas or in California—the Smoking Demon was right there with me. Like an idiot, I had thrown down the gauntlet that night in Las Vegas. This time, however, it was the Smoking Demon that was saying "Bring it on!"

Don't misunderstand me. I am not using this demon as an excuse for my continuing to smoke or going back to it. That, I confess, is entirely on me. I can truthfully say this, however: on a scale of difficulty ranging from 1 to 10, he made quitting a 15! Over the years, I had easily quit several times with no issues. This time though, was completely different. Perhaps because Sidekick was fully aware of the conflict the smoking caused between my husband and me.

I finally made the decision to return to my sister's at the end of January 2020 to launch Operation Quit-Smoking. Believe me, if anyone could keep me in line regarding smoking, it was my big sister. In fact, she and my mother had done a good bit of bonding over their mutual hatred of that habit! In our first book, *The Hauntings of Two Sisters—Shocking True Life Experiences,* I tell the story of how my dead mother appeared to me in my sister's backyard and told me how urgent it was that I quit. I was fortified by the same feeling of comfort and confidence I'd felt as a little girl when she tucked me in for my bedtime story. The moment she put her warm hand on my knee to let me know that all would be well, I promised her that I would. Quite honestly, though, it was just about the hardest promise I have ever tried to keep. %$#&ing Smoking Demon!

Okay, back to Operation Quit-Smoking. First off, I'm going to come clean. I smoked all the way from Las Vegas to California. I was panicking because of my impending divorce from my beloved habit! Disgusting, right? The good news is that my sister and I had a plan. She allowed me to smoke the first two weeks at her house, smoking less and less each day until I could survive four to five hours between cigarettes. From there, the next and final stop would (hopefully) be cold turkey! As it turned out (you know what the author said about best laid plans), the Smoking Demon was not quite done with me. For some reason, about a week after I had quit, my sister decided to check her backyard security cameras at four o'clock one morning. Weird in itself, right? What she saw there was me in my regular smoking spot, in my smoking coat, in her dimly lit yard puffing away on a cigarette. She only saw the side of my face though, and of course, it wasn't the real me she was looking at. Obviously, it was a trouble-making doppelganger but at the time, however, my sister was unaware of that. "Transforms into Different Images" (#6 on our Top Ten List) That explains those outbursts during which she let me have it for giving into those nicotine cravings after the plan had been in effect for only a week. So crazy!

I believe I did what many smokers who are trying to quit do: I grabbed a sucker and stuck it in my mouth every time I craved a cigarette. The first week I went through $30 worth of suckers and gained a few pounds for my efforts. It was hilarious but I did it! I had actually quit smoking. Even on the long nine-hour drive back to Las Vegas, I didn't crave or indulge myself with a cigarette even once! I was incredibly happy, having fulfilled my promise to my dead mother. From there it was five long and enjoyable months of non-smoking bliss! I told my husband that for Mother's Day I wanted a T-shirt that said "Quit" on the front, and on the back, it would say "cigarettes, sugar and drugs." The energy I had was nothing short of over-the-top incredible! It was as if I was 40 years old again. The Smoking Demon had completely vanished, and for my husband and I life was good! (Note: this was two months before Covid-19 hit and the entire nation shut down).

Unfortunately, because of all of his listening devices (in the house, the garage, the backyard and in our cars), Sidekick knew exactly how great my life was going. It didn't help that my daughter was always mentioning it to him.

Then it started happening. As if my recent success in my battle to quit smoking had never occurred, my cigarette cravings were back in force, thanks to the Smoking Demon and Sidekick! It seemed like he was out to insinuate himself into every nook and cranny of my life. That &^%$ demon was following me everywhere and was doing his best to penetrate into the deepest recesses of my psyche! I was stricken by a desperate need to smoke! I had never experienced this type of overpowering desire before, and it got so bad that smoking was all I could think about 24/7!

Sidebar: All of you smokers/former smokers out there know exactly what I am talking about. You always crave that gotta-have morning cigarette with your coffee and the one after dinner/before bed. My craving at this point, however, was so much more than that.

I gave myself a wee bit of credit for lasting an entire month before giving into these nerve-wracking urges. I began by having one cigarette a day, and that quickly turned into ten. I had a ready-made excuse. I was as bored as everyone else and needed something to do. The next thing to go was my self-esteem, as I found myself repeatedly reflecting on what a loser I was. To put it bluntly, my inner peace was gone!

It seemed like an eternity but finally my mother paid a timely visit from the other side. She clued me in to the fact that Sidekick had been performing nightly rituals on me for weeks to get me to start smoking again! Of all the things that Sidekick had done to me or tried to do to me over the previous 19 months (including killing me), this was the most unforgivable! One question above all kept pounding at my brain. When was I going to finally and once-and-for-all stop being his victim?

My dead mother and living sister continued to escalate things with their nonstop barrage of demands that I put the tobacco habit behind me. My sister was absolutely furious! Accompanying me on my quit-smoking effort all through January was hell on her, a fact that she impressed on me in no uncertain terms. As aware as she was of the battery of rituals Sidekick had been performing on/against me in order to release the Smoking Demon on me, her response remained, "Just fight it harder"!

The problem was that I am not superhuman!! The last few chapters have amply proved that, right? It ALL affects me in some way or another. My abiding thought was that Pam wasn't living with these demons and Sidekick 24/7 like I was. (Yes, I freely admit it, yet another excuse for my behavior.)

We decided to rent cabins for a four-day family vacation at California's Big Bear Lake. We could still isolate ourselves yet enjoy a much-needed change of scenery and some fresh mountain air. This break in our routine was badly needed after months of Covid-19 quarantine. My sister was still doing her full court press on my smoking habit, letting me know that either I refrain from smoking during our stay at the lake or we could make the trip without her. Yikes! The last thing I would ever want to do was to lie to her, so I made sure that I didn't promise anything more than I knew I could deliver. In this case, it was a promise that I would not light up in her presence. At the time, I don't think that she even noticed that my response was a bit on the cagey side. As it turned out, I was able to keep my promise, as difficult as it was for me. Although Smoking Demon was with me the entire time at Big Bear, I managed, nonetheless, not to smoke in front of my sister. (Note: I told her everything when I got back to Las Vegas.)

I know I must sound like an awful addict. I've been able to kick really bad addictions before, having gone cold turkey off opioids after 18 years of using. I was constantly reminding myself that I was stronger than this. But in reality, when it came to my battle against my Smoking Demon buddy, I really wasn't. Demons go after your greatest vulnerability, and by that time I had become all too aware of the fact that for me, that meant smoking.

Fast forward to the end of summer. I am at my sister's in California, making another serious attempt at quitting. Pam had decided to cut me a bit of slack regarding our stop-smoking campaign. She had agreed, in fact, to look the other way if I limited my smoking territory to my car, which I agreed to park down the street. There was one exception to this agreement. To help make sure that I was safe, if I was going to sit in my car and smoke after dark, she preferred that I parked my car right in front of her house. One morning at about 5:00, I was having a cigarette in my car. It was still dark and the driver's side door was open. I was sitting sideways, listening to my favorite morning show on XM radio. I just happened to glance up and see Smoking Demon walk out the front door of my sister's house and head across the lawn straight towards me. Even if I could show you a detailed illustration of that scene, it couldn't even begin to capture the "I own you" attitude—along with the cruel, mocking laughter, the smugness, the ugly arrogance and, ultimately, the hate I felt and saw coming from him that was beyond comprehension. I didn't even shut my car door. Instead, I just sat there almost paralyzed in my arrogance. He walked right up to the car—and vanished.

This may sound unbelievably stupid, considering how long it took me to see what I needed to see. At that moment, I finally realized that this demon had gained a debilitating degree of control over me. Strangely enough, I understood that this was a form of possession. It was a form that manifested itself as a demonic fog that chained me to a nicotine habit. It took me another extremely long and extremely difficult three weeks, but at last I was able to kick that Smoking Demon and my demon-fueled smoking habit to the curb. It had been a very scary experience for me, especially since he/it could have plugged into anything to which I was vulnerable: sex, liquor, hard drugs, you name it. That being said, I suppose that in a way I was lucky that I chose smoking as my area of vulnerability and not something that often kills many people before they even reach middle age. Even with the protection afforded me by my faith, I still let it in; I still let this happen.

Sidebar: It was the last time I ever told a demon, "Bring it on!"

See, none of us are superhuman!

15

OMG Can It
Get Any Worse

✝

Karen Pena

And so, the story continues. . . .

My thoughts on this chapter were, honestly, all over the place. My daily prayer to God has always been, "God grant me the wisdom I need." My prayer was fulfilled tenfold! My wisdom grew substantially from the following experiences.

To be overly dramatic and honest, I was hanging onto my daughter's soul and my own sanity with nothing more than daily prayer and sheer force of will! I kept telling myself if it costs me my life, it's completely worth it. I was not going to allow Satan and his Sidekick to have my daughter's soul. This goal was why I was getting up in the morning, why I was still breathing. This was the beginning and the end for me.

After our trip to Big Bear, the surreal conditions of my personal life amped up considerably. Sidekick's rituals and hate became exponentially more intense. On a very consistent basis, the demons were telling me to kill myself in multiple ways. Yes, at this time, of course, I was extremely emotionally vulnerable under the circumstances. However, I know myself very well and that included knowing my own thoughts. These were not my own thoughts at any time in my life. Whenever I would have them, I would simply laugh and say "Jesus" out loud to the demon, and the thoughts would go away immediately.

You have heard it all before in my previous chapters. I really don't want to sound like a broken record. I had come home from my sisters so strong physically, spiritually and mentally (Chapter 11 "I am Back and Stronger"). Obviously to me, the months of demonic oppression in the house had taken its toll on me in all aspects of my being. Now the more pressing and serious concern was my diabetes. My sugars were running 400-600 24/7 no matter what I did to try to control them. You're not going to believe this, but my carbohydrate intake (which is one of the factors that causes high sugars) was below 10 carbs a day. This should have translated to lower sugar levels. The high sugars were causing chaos to my body. My dead mother gave my sister a message: If I didn't get my sugars down immediately, I was going to have a stroke. In addition, she said I needed to have my kidneys examined. When I went to the doctor, he didn't believe that my carb intake was so limited. I actually screamed at him, "You have to believe me so we can come up with a solution!" His solution was to prescribe high quantities of insulin. All it did was put 27 pounds of weight on me in two months but still didn't control my sugars. My sister, a serious diabetic, kept telling me you must have an infection somewhere in your body, that's the only answer. I agreed with her. However, after many medical tests, nothing was found.

I know that there are people reading this right now that understand my sense of helplessness. I am not the only person in this world that has gone through a serious battle between good and evil. In my soul, I knew it was just another way for Satan, his Sidekick and his minions to attack my health. I was feeling that same evil energy again. The same energy I felt before my sister came to Las Vegas to retrieve me and eventually save my life. Even though I had fought so incredibly hard, I had demonic attachments again. I was so focused on my daughter's well-being that I wasn't properly protecting myself.

One summer afternoon, I had a rare moment where I was alone in the house. I was taking advantage of it by quietly sitting in my bedroom writing. Boom! The loudest noise I had ever heard in the house came from above me upstairs. Boom! There it went again. I immediately called my sister to tell her and then another Boom! She heard it also. I ran to my bedroom door, slammed it shut and locked it. I wasn't thinking an intruder. I was thinking a big powerful demon! Maybe a ZoZo! For those unaware, a ZoZo is a very violent and dangerous demonic entity. Who knew with Sidekick, right? Just then I heard solid footsteps walking through the kitchen which was adjacent to my bedroom door. It didn't sound like the hooves of a ZoZo but the feet of a big man. I quietly sat there with my sister on the phone waiting to see what would happen next. My heart was pounding while my mouth was open, sucking in shallow breaths.

Then I saw it.

The shadow of a man or a demon, something, underneath my bedroom door, walking back and forth then stopping in front of my door. The knob began to jiggle. Immediately, I cut my sister off and dialed 911. I was on the phone with the 911 operator while looking at the shadow moving back and forth underneath the door. I explained to her exactly what was happening. Within minutes, the police were at the front door. When the doorbell rang, the shadow underneath the door disappeared. I stiffened my spine, opened the bedroom door and made a run for the front door. When I opened it, there stood seven of the largest police officers on the Vegas force I had ever seen! I have no idea what warranted receiving so many police, but what the hell. Who am I to argue? On my tippy toes, I glanced over their shoulders and saw seven huge SUVs perfectly lined up on the street behind each other with the entire neighborhood outside watching.

I was asked to stay outside. The largest cop was left to protect me while the other six went into the house with guns drawn.

After 20 intense minutes of searching the house, are you surprised when I tell you the police found NOTHING!

When the police left, and I had made some reassuring comments to our neighbors. I thought long and hard about what had just occurred. I kept asking myself over and over why would I automatically assume it was a human being in the house when for months I knew it was demons? Simple answer: because they wanted me to believe it was a human intruder so I would look bat shit crazy again to my family and now my neighbors. I could hear it now: "Karen's really lost it this time!" Strangely enough, my daughter came home, took me aside and said, "You know it was demons messing with you, right?" (*2 Corinthians 2:11 "In order that Satan might not outwit us. For we are not unaware of his schemes."*)

Ok, the lessons continue.

A week went by. Sidekick had a complete meltdown for another meaningless reason, stormed out of the house, got in his truck and burned rubber.

I knew immediately something bad was going to happen. Maybe someone was telling me from the other side. I don't know. I just knew someone was going to get hurt from his crazy, out-of-control, emotional driving. Right then my sister calls and tells me the same thing. My dead mother had filled her in on what was going on. We prayed together and waited.

An hour later, the front door banged open. He stormed in, angrier than he was when he left. I was cooking dinner, thinking that's not good. He begun by talking really fast (high on something?) which is typical when he's in an unstable, volatile state of emotion or on drugs.

Apparently, he was driving erratically and enraged when he rear-ended another truck. For whatever reason, the truck he hit took off immediately. However, his truck was badly damaged in the front, and inoperable.

Weeks later, Sidekick had another temper tantrum or meltdown, whatever you want to call it. I've had to come up with all sorts of synonyms in the last 19 months for how he behaves. This time he ran out to the desert beyond our house. Hours later, he came busting through the front door, hooping and howling in pain. Apparently, he was running through the desert full of overwhelming anger when he fell into a prairie hole. Some people just never learn, do they? Or maybe it's Karma. Even as I am writing this, I am laughing so hard tears are in the corners of my eyes. I realize this is not a good reaction. But, in my defense, I had been tortured by him and his minions for so long and all I could think was, "What goes around comes around." Unfortunately, this applied to me as well.

The following day I was talking to my sister on the phone. I was recounting the prairie hole incident when I began to laugh uncontrollably. This time laughter tears were rolling effortlessly down my face. You have already read the chapter "Can you hear me now?" Therefore, you are aware that he could hear my laughter when he eventually listened back to the recordings of our private phone conversation.

The following morning, I woke up with serious left wrist pain. I never hurt my wrist, never had any chronic conditions with my wrist. But out of nowhere, agony! I was disabled and in terrible pain for over five months. Am I saying Sidekick performed a ritual and had a demon do this? Yes! No doubt! That is exactly what I am saying and what happened.

Again, some people just never learn.

Myself included.

16

Tug-of-War
of the Soul

✝

Karen Pena

It's a beautiful warm Saturday morning in Las Vegas and I am sitting out in my truck in the parking lot of Albertson's supermarket, finishing up a cigarette and getting ready to do some much-needed grocery shopping. That's when the voice came to me. A clear, strong male not-at-all-unfamiliar voice that I'd heard at other critical junctures in my life and had no trouble recognizing in the supermarket parking lot. Its message, as always, was blessedly simple: "It is time. It is time for Jennifer to get on her knees and turn her heart over to me." It was God's voice, and I was as shocked, surprised and just plain awed by it as I was the first time, I'd heard it.

Allow me to give you, the reader, some background leading up to this moment.

My daughter had always believed in God, like many people do, but He wasn't a priority in her life. Over the last 19 months, however, this subject had become much more urgent to the two of us. Up to this point, the love of her life was Sidekick, a Satan worshiper. Initially, she was in denial about it. But over the last few months, too many dots were starting to connect themselves for her to deny it any longer. Our discussions on the subject of God had gone up several notches in both frequency and intensity, and we both prayed every day that God would intervene and save Sidekick. On one occasion, Sidekick was having yet another meltdown and warning me with a super-loud scream that he was going to be high up in Hell—yada yada yada—at the same time God was also communicating to me. He said He couldn't save Sidekick because he would not meet him halfway. I told my daughter what God had said. But her response clued me in to the fact that she still was in denial and still held out hope that God would step in and change Sidekick's life for the better.

It was so obvious to me that my daughter's soul was being used as a Tug-of-War between myself and Sidekick.

He wanted her to join him in worshiping the dark side and I wanted her to give her heart to God. At times, I felt her being pulled so far into the Demonic Fog that I was afraid she would not be able to see her way out of it, that I was losing my grip on my side of the tug-of-War rope! But God wasn't going to give up and neither was I. My sister and I intensified our prayers hoping to change the direction of that Tug-of-War game that Sidekick and I were playing. We truly believed that God was in it to win it!

Through daily prayer and involvement in the horror of this on-going situation with her boyfriend, she began to rely more and more on God. Her daily periods of communion with Him got longer and stronger. And then it arrived. God's "it is time" message arrived the same morning on which my daughter and I had a beautiful conversation about His truly amazing grace. We were in the backyard, just she and I speaking about God's love and grace, when we both looked up and there was Sidekick watching us intently from the master bedroom window. His face was distorted with hate. We both waved at him, laughing out loud. We didn't get a wave back.

So, I am in the parking lot of Albertson's when God gives me the message for my daughter. Immediately after receiving it, I texted Jennifer the exact words that God spoke out loud to me. I told her to go to a very private spot where she can't be bothered by anyone (in our house that's the bathroom) and, if she's willing, give her heart to God.

She did get on her knees and gave her heart to God.

Everything in the house changed in an instant, and

immediately, God lifted the Demonic Fog that had imprisoned her for so long. He took "ALL" of Sidekick's evil mojo out of her in a second, mojo that had probably taken him years of rituals to place in her.

This happened on Saturday morning, and by Tuesday, right after Sidekick's encore meltdown, she finally gave him his marching orders. Of course, the coward refused to leave, even when the police asked him to. But that's another chapter. The point is, my daughter was at last aware of what was going on, focused herself accordingly and started working on getting him out as soon as possible! The tides were turning.

After over 19 months of literal hell, God made it all seem so simple. He was in it to win it now. Was this all about my daughter's soul in the long run? If so, it was all worthwhile.

The
Meltdowns

✝

Karen Pena

THE MELTDOWNS
(OR THE BEGINNING OF THE END)

Early one Thursday morning, I woke up in a great mood. I was leaving the veterinarian's office at about a quarter after seven after dropping off my little toy fox terrier puppy, Kiki (she was being spayed), when I received a text from my daughter. It read, "When you come home, ignore Sidekick, he's in one of his moods." I thought to myself, "Crap!" Another day of walking on eggshells—a description that was, as I soon found out, an understatement.

When I walked in through the back door, the demon oppression was overwhelming. I could easily make out three of them scurrying around the living room. Their rumpus was accompanied by a sound coming from upstairs of objects shattering against the walls and floor. It didn't stop there, though. This exceedingly unrelentless, ear-splitting racket was underscored by the sound of Sidekick screaming at the top of his lungs, seemingly to an invisible audience. His performance left my dog Cash cowering in the corner and trembling with fear. It was extremely embarrassing for my daughter who, at that time, was on a work call in her home office. Very concerned about what all this was doing to my poor pooch, I told my daughter via text message that Sidekick's behavior was unacceptable and that she needed to step in and lay down the law to him. Not at all happy about having her work interrupted, she stomped out of her office, the anger coming off her in waves so thick you could have cut them with a dull knife. She screamed, "Calm the fuck down!" at him. Wow. I mean double, triple, quadruple wow! I have never, ever heard my daughter yell like that before. Unfortunately, however, it was all the encouragement Sidekick needed to start screaming vile, awful slanderous things in return. Among these were promises to haunt her the rest of her life and to make sure that she never enjoyed a moment's peace again. The torture to which he was subjecting her was altogether brutal, and I felt tortured as well by being powerless to help.

Cash, Karen's Pitbull

As they stood there continuing to scream at each other, the fight escalated. I ran into my bedroom, pulled my 9mm gun out from underneath my pillow and removed it from the holster. After locking and loading it, I dialed 911 on my phone so that all I would have to do was to press the call button if things continued to go downhill. Minutes turned into hours and ended up taking up a good part of the day. Cash and I sat there as jittery as jittery can be waiting to see if my daughter needed armed intervention. Simply put, I was terrified, and a jumble of other emotions flowed through me like flood waters gone wild. Finally, I got tired of waiting. I texted her and told her I was going to call 911. My sister agreed with my decision and pleaded with me to do it immediately. My daughter, though, begged me not to for fear that they would 5150 him (haul him in for a psychiatric evaluation). She reasoned that this would lead to an entirely different set of problems, that Sidekick would see it as an inexcusable betrayal and come after her with incredible revenge.

Evidently, Sidekick had decided that it was time for Act II. The drama continued with him taking the action outside and treating our neighbor to a great big helping of yell-power. He then sprinted back into the house, where he proceeded to start cleaning the kitchen as noisily as possible while screaming at the top of his lungs to no one in particular (himself maybe?) the entire time. It was bizarre yet familiar, it hardly being the first time he has acted in this manner. This time, however, there was a new element as the language he was speaking morphed from English into some foreign-sounding gibberish. Apparently, he was giving a piece of his mind to only God knows who or what was listening.

Okay, it's full confession time here. This actually freaked me out more than anything else in that morning's cavalcade of shit. He made sure to enhance the day's festivities with a thoroughly psychotic bang, breaking the garbage disposal, the dual recycle/garbage can and the recently installed gate that blocked off the stairs from the dogs—all within minutes! Unbelievable!

After all that, we still weren't even close to being done. More drama was on the way. My son was due at the house at 11:00 am that morning, and I quickly called him to tell him not to come. The last thing I wanted was for him to walk into this hellish mess and get involved in it in any way, shape or form. I felt that I owed him an explanation for urging him to cancel his visit, and after I explained the situation to him, he was furious! I knew that would be his reaction, and that is precisely why I needed him to stay away from the house that day. My men came through like princes, with my son calling me every hour on the hour just to make sure that his sister and I were alright, and my husband texting me every half hour to see if there was anything he could do to help. (Oh yea, come home.) My sister didn't ease up either in the love-and-support department, and even though she was up to her ears in a multitude of audits, she stayed on the phone with me throughout the day.

Having gotten a taste of the verbal and emotional abuse to which Sidekick had already subjected my daughter, we were just waiting for the proverbial other shoe to drop. At that point, we were all sure of three things. Eventually his abuse would turn violent, this new phase would begin soon, and today could be the day. Meanwhile, his mega-meltdown went on, and as morning became afternoon and evening approached, he was still going at it. I had learned to be ultra-cautious where this man was concerned, and was careful not to underestimate how much danger my daughter was in. I knew darn well that I could scarcely afford the luxury of letting down my guard even for a second. Fortunately, I had the advantage of having access to another pair of eyes and ears to monitor our boy's movements in the house, during his meltdown. Jennifer was notifying me via text message any time Sidekick came downstairs or when he went back up. Since my poor doggie Cash was so upset by this time that he would not eat or take his medicine, I had to make repeated visits to the kitchen to experiment with different kinds of food for him. Then my daughter's text arrived.

"Lock yourself in your bedroom and don't come out! He's exploding with anger and it's all targeted at you!" Then it got even worse. I was in the kitchen, busy trying to get Cash to take his medicine. At first there was some good news . . . finally! Cash seemed to be recovering from all that stress. With one eye I saw him roll on his back and heard him make a noise that I learned when he was younger was his happy sound. Suddenly, out of the other eye, I could see the outline of a big black dog sitting next to the couch while treating me to a laser-focused stare. I was confused. I looked at Cash, reminding myself that I had only one big dark dog, and that was him. Then my entire focus shifted back to the other dog. I turned my head to look at it again, and what I saw made my jaw drop. Sitting there was the largest Doberman Pinscher I'd ever seen. He stood least four feet tall from floor to the tips of his ears. His chest was truly massive, and oddly enough, an actual name tag hung down from his thick brown collar! While I stood there staring at him, utterly transfixed by his appearance, he returned the favor by fixing me with his coal-black eyes. What the hell? Looking back on that moment, my guess is that his next move—vanishing into thin air—took place at the exact moment that he knew that I had registered him in my mind. Now I knew that there was yet another hellhound in the house who was interested in me (hellhound number three, coming right up). The question was, did this one also come with a demon owner? Are they taking advantage of my love and affection for dogs?

I knew exactly why he was focused on me and I followed my daughter's instructions about securely locking myself in my room. A few minutes later, more help came my way in the form of a message from the other side, a message that could not have been more serious. My dead mother warned me that Sidekick was going to bait me into abandoning the safety of my room so that he could cause me physical harm! Strangely enough, when he came downstairs, he was telling someone with whom he was talking on his cellphone that I had pointed a loaded gun at him. After letting the listener know that "it may take me a few years to get revenge against her, but I WILL get my revenge," he went on to make a number of horrible accusations against my daughter!

I was angry! I was just about to walk out there and confront him about these inexcusable lies when I stopped. Was Mom's warning spot on? Was he baiting me? Was he trying to set me up so he would be justified in hurting me? After my mother signaled her agreement to this interpretation by shouting "yes!!!" in a very loud voice, I figured I'd better stay in my locked room with my gun ready. His attempt to bait me into stepping out into the hallway, where he would have a clear line of attack, went on for the next two hours. I sat there shaking with rage and frustration; I kept saying to myself over and over again, "This is crazy!"

His tantrum lasted the entire day, only ending when my husband rode his motorcycle into the garage at a quarter after five. Right before hubby came into the house, Sidekick walked upstairs, and we didn't see him again that night. Thank God. My daughter, Pam and I were emotionally drained. My fibromyalgia was acting up and once again, my sugars were out of control. I was tired, so tired that I couldn't even begin to process what had just happened. As much as I would like to give you, the reader, an accurate picture of Sidekick's meltdown, I'm afraid that no words could begin to truly express the terror that filled just about every single moment of that day.

Later that night, my daughter texted me to tell me that she had heard a loud growl outside her bedroom window. She thought it must have been an enormous coyote coming in from the desert. That explanation didn't make much sense in view of the fact that she was on the second floor and all her windows were closed. I knew from my late-night smoking breaks in the backyard that the coyotes never came into the neighborhood. If they did, they would have run in large packs. I also knew that she'd had an encounter with the huge hellhound that I'd seen that day, the Doberman pincher. I had heard that loud growl before in many different spots in the house: garage, kitchen, laundry room, stairs, living room, loft and my own bedroom.

Sidekick's foul (and just plain evil) mood lasted through Saturday, although he was extremely careful how much anger he showed around Oscar. Late Saturday night, two factors came into play. First, my dead mother appeared with another urgent and possibly life-saving message. She informed me that it was no longer safe for me to stay in that house and that I should leave for my sister's place right away, in fact, the next morning. Second, and so very personally touching for me, my daughter came to our room late that night and told me it was no longer safe for me there. I needed to leave for my sister's as soon as possible until she can get Sidekick out of the house permanently!

OMG FINALLY! THIS IS HUGE! Nineteen months of torture, dealing with the Top Ten List, the hellhounds, the mental, physical and spiritual sacrifice, thousands of hours of prayer involving so many gracious people, the incredible efforts from my dead family on the other side, the Archangel Michael, the protection of angels and finally our amazing and loving God. No Rosemary's baby! I left at 4:00 am the next (Sunday) morning, September 20, 2020.

Once I arrived at my sister's, even though I was on my knees thanking the Almighty, I was also dreadfully aware of my daughter's overwhelming sense of sadness and hurt. To her, at the moment, he was the love of her life, a relationship that lasted off and on in excess of 20 years. Through my incredible relief, my heart was in turmoil for my daughter. There's a big HOWEVER here though: I knew she would eventually refocus her inner health to a wonderful man who would be incredibly worthy of her. Out with the Satan worship! Again, she had no concept what Sidekick was about and what he was capable of. A few months ago, God allowed me to view a video in my psyche surrounding how many lives Sidekick had negatively influenced and ruined. What can I possibly say? The video took my breath away. There was so much agony, so much pain. My thoughts, where there had to be purpose in God permitting Sidekick to continue but unfortunately, I am only able to see the chaotic side of the tapestry.

The following Tuesday, I received a frantic call from my daughter. Sidekick was having another meltdown, but this time it was unique. This time my daughter felt fear; she knew she could possibly be in physical danger. Finally, she was experiencing exactly what I felt each and every time Sidekick erupted! A barrier had definitely fragmented amongst the two of them (thank you, God) but this time I wasn't there to protect her, no one was. We had a safe word; if she texted it to me then I immediately dialed 911. I sat quietly by my phone for 3 hours, not moving, praying once again that she would be safe.

I am sharing a horrible episode in a series of so many traumatic stages. I desperately need to take a moment and a deep breath to explain to you, as the reader, the contemplations, judgments and beliefs going around and around in my exhausted head. So much fear that he would finally, after 19 months, extract from me what I treasured most, my daughter. I had an anger so overwhelming that I feared it would cost me my salvation! My head was spinning with the unceasing question I kept asking myself over and over again, whenever the reality of the situation would settle over me: how could this be happening?

However, my daughter had undergone an emotional metamorphosis. God had cleansed her of all the bad mojo or spells that Sidekick had layered over her fragile heart and soul over the years. At last, she had clarity!_Sidekick had decisively miscalculated her born-again experience with God and the effect it had on who she was becoming.

She waited until her dad and brother were surrounding her and then bravely placed a call to the police department to have Sidekick escorted out of the house permanently. Then they waited.

Oh, if life was that easy right? When the two police officers went upstairs, Sidekick had locked himself in the master bedroom. (Coward with a four-letter word in front of it!) He spoke to the officers through the door, telling them that he had lived there for almost 18 months. He showed them proof of residency. You know exactly what I am going to say next. There was nothing the police could do. My daughter would have to file with the courts and legally evict him which could take months.

After the police left, Sidekick barricaded himself in the master bedroom, having pushed the large dresser up against the bedroom door.

The next day my husband phoned to ask me if I could look up hotel rooms for him with weekly rates! What the hell, I thought! I was physically and mentally tortured by that despicable person for 18 months; I remained for my husband, my dog and my daughter! Yes, my husband was a formidable skeptic. Nonetheless as my sister had stated many times, "Take the Satan worship plus demons out of it and you still have a horrific situation." He's a person who doesn't want to work, an unstable, volatile person who is high as a kite 24/7, a thief with a serious case of hate, revenge and PTSD. When you stare it in the face, is there really a choice?

My money-conscious husband did make the decision to remain at the house. However, he was at work the entire day. Therefore, my precious daughter designated her working time at a friend's. She and her dad would meet in front of her house so they could enter together. Every night when my husband walked in the house, Sidekick was already barricaded in the master bedroom.

Was the Satan worshiper actually afraid of my husband? He had no trouble at all hurting a 60-year-old woman along with her sister. Personally, I found this to be a laugh-out-loud moment.

This routine continued day after day until eventually, my daughter felt safe enough working at home again. I wanted to go home desperately to protect my daughter, but God had clearly told me that HE would take care of the situation. Therefore, with my heart breaking, I stayed in California, waiting for the grateful day I could see my family again.

Weeks went by. Seriously. I stayed quiet, allowing my daughter and husband to deal with the move out. When I did inquire about the situation, I was told Sidekick had a list of issues to deal with before he could exit our lives. For example, truck registration, insurance, etc., issues my daughter had been attempting to get him to complete for almost two years.

Meanwhile, my daughter was working at home, in the front office, mostly with the door locked, and Sidekick had the house to himself. At this point, there was no communication between the two of them. But here's an interesting note. She called me and said that Sidekick was anxiously pacing the house yelling things like, "Fuck you,

Jehovah" and "I hate God." Do you believe he took my discussion on accountability to heart? Or was this about my daughter's salvation and her metamorphosis?

Finally, she asked him what was happening. This was interesting also. He said to leave him alone, that he was dealing with a "mystic halo." It was such an odd expression, of course I googled it immediately! I felt it was a bit of proof with my daughter since the internet explained the expression had something to do with Satan worship. Scary!

18

Safe Zone

✝

Pam Mandel

I felt so relieved that my sister was now safe and secure with me. With many miles between Sidekick and her, I felt the damage was restricted only to the outcome of his daily sorcery rituals. That by itself can be devastating; however, even with all the demons and their pets he sends our way, the feeling of him being that far away seemed comforting to both of us. There was a big difference between being in the same house with him or in another state. For one thing, the 24/7 depression and oppression were absent.

For weeks, our dead mom had been telling me that Karen needed to leave the house of horrors (Hell's sublet). But now that things were escalating with the tantrums and meltdowns on a day-to-day basis, Karen's daughter was also agreeing with our dead mom. You see, since Karen's daughter, Jennifer, had given her heart to God, Sidekick was furious. His hate for my sister was now off the charts.

Karen's husband was still in a Demonic Fog. He wasn't on board with this like we all were. Karen was starting to take more of a stand with him. She was hoping he would finally realize they needed to move out of their daughter's home. Her health, be it mental, physical or spiritual, depended on it.

The night before my sister was starting her road trip to my home, my dead mom reached out to me. She encouraged me to meet her part of the way. Knowing how hard a nine-hour drive was for one person, my husband and I decided it was a good idea. My sister was packed up for a long stay with us, bringing both hot and cold weather clothes. In addition, she had her two dogs with her.

As the situation with Sidekick escalated, my sister felt helpless and very concerned with the safety of both her husband and daughter. Due to the pandemic, her daughter worked from home behind a locked door during the day while her husband went to his office. At least during the evenings, they would be together.

Karen and I encouraged Jennifer to start the eviction process, however she wanted to handle the situation with Sidekick's eviction her way, allowing him to take all the time he needed to prepare for his long-awaited departure. OMG, Karen and I knew exactly what that meant. Time for him to line up his ducks and in our minds, this could mean disaster. Time to install more listening devices, cameras, bad mojo and more devastating ways to re-enter the home. We didn't agree with her, but Karen was just happy that things were headed in the right direction. Satan's Sidekick was moving out!

With all the listening devices planted, he was hearing everything that was going on. It didn't matter if we were talking in the home or car. Somehow, he knew exactly what we were up to. This made it next to impossible for any communication between my sister, her husband and daughter. Eventually Jennifer got a second phone and started calling my husband's cellphone (which was a safe zone) so she could speak to Karen. Definitely it was a little convoluted at times.

Not knowing how long the situation would take, I spoke to Karen about regrouping, setting much-needed priorities while she was staying with us. Hoping to get her mind off the problematic situation by focusing on constructive things.

We set goals for my sister in the order below:
- Work on getting her diabetics under control.
- Quit smoking.
- Have much-needed dental work done.

- Spiritual Healing and Cleansing.
- Train her new puppy Kiki.
- Working together to finish our second book.
- Getting ready for the upcoming Holidays.

As we moved forward with the above goals, it seemed like time was moving forward with no progress. Three weeks had gone by and Sidekick still had not vacated the premises. My sister's frustration was growing along with her homesickness. She was really missing her husband, kids and grandkids, and it was getting harder and harder for her to stay away from them all. Karen asked her daughter how much longer, but she didn't have an answer. Meanwhile, Sidekick was hitting it out of the park with his nightly horrors aimed at my sister. He was sending powerful demons into her room on a nightly basis, overwhelming her with negativity.

At one point, Karen went through a period of intense dreams of every possible scenario. These dreams vacillated from Sidekick beating her to actually killing her. This horror went on every night for over a week. There was one night when we both thought we saw him in the house. But with so many miles between us, how could that be?

One night I was awakened around 2:00 am and heard a dog on the other side of my bedroom door, crying and scratching. I immediately called her on her cell and asked her, "Why are your dogs at my bedroom door?" She said both her dogs were on her bed asleep! So what dog was it? I got up and opened the door and you guessed it—no dog! A few nights later, the same thing transpired. This time I immediately got up and opened the door—again, no dog! What was going on?

Karen and Pam's dogs

Now it even got beyond mystifying. I was sleeping and heard a noise in our bedroom. I opened my eyes and saw my sister walking from my husband's side of the bed and out the bedroom door. It was 1:00 in the morning. I asked her what she needed, thinking maybe an Advil. She didn't answer but continued out the bedroom door. I got up and went to her bedroom and, low and behold, she was sound asleep. Spooky, huh? This was the second time I had seen my sister's doppelganger. "Transforms into Different Images" (#6 on our Top Ten List)

Later that week, my sister's husband phoned me because he wanted to surprise her for their 32nd wedding anniversary on October 22, 2020. Knowing how much she missed him, I was excited for her. Yes, I kept my mouth shut so she would be surprised. He arrived on October 21st and she was just thrilled. They celebrated in San Francisco at her much-loved restaurant on the Wharf.

That night around 1:00 am, my husband and I were hastily awakened by the sound of the shutters on the patio door repetitively hitting the wall, followed by a noise-defying crash. We dashed into the living room only to find complete silence. There was no sign of anything or anyone that could account for the noise. We were both taken aback by this. A couple hours later I was again awakened, however this time by a creepy sensation. I sat up looking straight ahead and standing in the corner was the huge eight-foot demon, staring directly at me. As soon as I saw it, it disappeared!

During the time my sister's husband was visiting her, their daughter stayed with a friend, which left Sidekick secluded in the house for days. You got it. Sidekick still occupied the house!

There were two other mind-boggling occurrences that transpired during this period. They were so implausible that we decided to give them their own chapters: Chapter 19 "The Day My Puppy Changed" and Chapter 20 "And Then There Was Dino."

There was a positive side to the several months she spent with us. All seven of our goals were achieved! My sister quit smoking on November 4, 2020 just before she began the reconstruction of her teeth.

The Day My
Puppy Changed

✝

Karen Pena

Again, another incident that occurred during the "Safe Zone." At this point, as far as I'm concerned, the name of that particular chapter is beginning to come into question.

During that time, I was having in-depth oral surgeries every Wednesday, week after week. Honestly, it was totally kicking my ass. Having said that, I was having problems saying my nightly prayers.

One evening while quietly listening to a podcast in bed, my little puppy, Kiki, was curled into me fast asleep. All of a sudden, she sat up abruptly in bed, staring at the bedroom doorway. I immediately turned my head to see what she was looking at. That is when I saw a stocky black silhouette raise its arm, pointing it directly at Kiki. Something like a piece of wire, similar to a stun gun, shot out from its finger over to my puppy. She literally jumped back as if something had hit her! I instantly grabbed her, thoroughly checked her out, and everything seemed fine. I would soon find out this was not the case.

First, let me give you a little backup information: Kiki adores me. She follows mommy everywhere. When she cannot find me, she becomes very agitated, running from room to room in a frenzy. This may consist of jumping on window sills, the back of chairs and sofas, with only one goal in mind: find Mommy. I guess you could say she's completely dependent on me, physically and emotionally. She is the type of puppy that wakes up happy, loving, hungry and very wild. Then she takes off to play with the other dogs, her pack. Just a delightful, little crazy toy fox terrier.

Within minutes, I noticed a difference immediately. She was confused, disorientated, and more importantly, she wanted nothing to do with me, running from me every time I sought her out. She would then stop, look at me and give me one of those long intense stares. I got the feeling she was fearful. It was this fear in her eyes that was unnerving; my dog was literally afraid of me.

I tried for hours but simply could not get Kiki into my bedroom to go to sleep. That night, she ended up sleeping with my sister and her husband in their bed with the dogs.

The next morning, she still did not want anything to do with the other dogs either, sprinting away from all who came close to her. And are you ready for this? She would not even eat. Trust me on this fact: Kiki lives for food! This dog is a real foodie, so that was very concerning for all of us.

Now even Pam and Michael were detecting a difference! They were getting concerned but thought she would snap out of it.

About 1:00 in the afternoon, Michael, my sister's husband, started yelling, "There's something really wrong with Kiki!" When I went out there where they were, she was FROZEN, standing there with her head down about five inces from the floor, staring at God knows what for a good half hour and not moving. Even when we called her name, she would not move. Was she in some sort of a trance? Was she slipping into another dimension? Pam said, "I think we need to take her to emergency immediately!" As afraid as I was for my tiny baby, I had seen what that demon had done the night before with his finger. What if Sidekick just wanted me to panic, spend thousands of dollars on tests at the emergency vet, and Kiki is just temporarily possessed?

I told Pam and Michael that I wanted to wait until the following morning before we reacted in any way. I had left over pain pills from her being spayed but as far as I could see, she was not in any pain. "Let's just wait," I kept saying. I prayed that I was not making a BIG mistake.

The day/night went on and the situation had not improved; Kiki was still acting 180 degrees from her normal sweet self. It was 10 pm, and by then I was totally convinced that my dog was unquestionably possessed. I could see Sidekick getting some sort of sick comfort out of this.

That night, Pam was able to get Kiki to sleep with me even though she did not want to. She was hoping this would help her to trust me again. Even though I did not have anything to do with what happened, I believe she was blaming me.

The following morning, Kiki was completely back to

normal, darting around the house looking for Mommy. She came back into my room, jumped on the bed full of hugs and kisses! I was so relieved and happy. However, I learned yet another valuable lesson in that 24-hour period. Now when I say my prayers, I make sure my animals are included.

To this day, none of us have a clue as to what took place with my puppy. Can animals become possessed? What we witnessed gives this thought credence.

20

And Then
There was Dino

✝

Karen Pena

Try to think of the weirdest looking animal you could ever imagine, making the craziest communication sounds possible. Then imagine this animal appearing in your bedroom out of nowhere!

This incident occurred during the "Safe Zone" and however, as weird, strange and out of this world as the experience was, I really felt it needed its own story. Out of ALL the circumstances in the last two years, this is the one I can't get out of my mind. But it happened to me and as you read on, my sister as well! You will probably think I truly am crazy, but I'm telling you it did happen.

One morning I was sitting on my bed, watching my morning show, while relishing my Puerto Rican java. Out of the corner of my right eye, I saw an unnatural movement. I turned to look and what I saw I'm still not sure if I should have been terrified, entertained, or break out with laughter. I will let you, the reader, determined that.

In the doorway of my bedroom was what I first believed to be a large ghost duck (I could see through it), spinning so fast on the tile that my eyes couldn't completely focus on it. On either side of this outrageous creature were two smaller furry animals that I could not make out. I knew these side show additions weren't important. The star of this twisted scenario was the spinner. Ok, what the hell is going on, right? What ritualistic spell brought this vision straight out of Hell and into our dimension? I'm telling you; you can't make this stuff up. At least I couldn't if I tried. I'm not creative enough.

I wanted to laugh, but I felt the evil energy and purpose radiating from it as it spun. At last, it was still and staring right at me! Literally, my mouth dropped opened looking back at whatever this was. Then the damn creature extended its long neck. Now I could clearly see that the skin was smooth (no feathers) and there was no beak, like a brontosaurus. It had flush wings tucked into its sides upfront on its body.

My favorite cartoon as a child was the Flintstones. I immediately yelled, "Dino!" Then it began to speak some sort of alien gibberish, only vowel sounds, each one a different voice reflection. As I previously said, I don't have the imagination to come up with this crazy stuff.

I ran down the hall to the living room where my sister was sitting. I couldn't get it out fast enough, what I had seen! She looked at me and said, "Karen you're being affected by the pain pills you're taking for your teeth." It was so crazy, she had me doubting myself and thinking maybe she's right, maybe it was a drug-induced hallucination. The reality was I saw the phantasm of this creature several more times that day! Was this something straight out of Hell or some kind of godly pet. The evil energy that I felt seemed to indicate the former.

One morning two weeks later, my sister came out of her bedroom, looked at me and said, "I'm sorry I doubted you, I thought you were crazy, but I saw Dino last night next to my bed!" My sister does not take drugs of any kind, much less hallucinogenic. She was sound asleep when the alien gibberish talk woke her up. Silently lying in bed listening to the unfamiliar sounds, she sat up and there it was! Right next to her bed, just a foot away, staring straight at her.

I am calling a shout out to all of you readers. Please contact us on our website: www.thehauntingsoftwosisters.com, if any of you have any knowledge or have ever seen anything like this before. I am desperate to know its purpose. To this day, I haven't a clue to what that might had been.

DEMON BLOCK

The last week of February 2021 was full of uneasy cold nights where I felt so uncomfortable and at times a little uneasy. I was constantly waking up with a start! After sitting up, I would spot a very large dark shadow man in the corner of my bedroom standing flat against the bright white bedroom door. I was blocked for the entire week from writing after being so tired during the days from no sleep at night.

21

The Move Out

✝

Karen Pena

I should make this apparent to you. My daughter booted Sidekick to the curb not because he was a Satan worshiper but because he was crazy! She has often asked me how can I know something is real if I can't see it? OK, it's called faith; you believe in God. Yet you haven't seen Him or have any concrete proof of Him except in your heart. I guess it was lack of belief in me just like my husband. It all just sounded so outrageous, bizarre, ridiculous. I could go on and on. My daughter's love of her life happens to be a Satan worshiper who's repeatedly tried to kill me. Just writing that gave me a laugh-out-loud, surreal moment. I understand completely the lack of belief.

After my daughter aided Sidekick in completing everything that he needed to do to exit our lives, he moved out on November 2, 2020.

At this point, I had been living in California for six weeks. I desperately wanted to take a moment to cherish the thought that it was finally over, that this particular evil has exited our lives for good. However, in reality, a new journey of nasty wickedness was just beginning. Sidekick was in phase two of his vile agenda for my friends and family.

The night of November 2nd is when the eight-foot demon first walked out of the gates of Hell and into our reality. My sister's ceilings are ten feet tall and his head stood a few inches above the top of the windows which are eight feet high. He had three-foot-wide shoulders, long legs and the shadows of muscles everywhere. He was the perfect definition of #2 on our Top Ten List for demons. He was in a sense, full out intimidation!

Initially, it manifested in Pam's room. She was in a deep sleep when she was suddenly awakened by a strange feeling. She sat up and there it was, just staring at her. They stared at each other for what seemed like minutes, when only seconds had gone by. She made a gesture to him and it quickly disappeared. Then "eight-footer" walked down the hall to my room. Lucky me!

I too was sound asleep. I quickly woke up with a gasp, while sitting up at the same time. For whatever reason, I looked straight at it. Standing unworldly still, an enormous demon statue leaned against the tall white door. It took a slight step to the right when I sat up and gasped, and then it disappeared. I glanced at the clock and, stereotypically, it was 3:00 am exactly. It was the time known as the witching hour or in our case, the demon hour.

Unfortunately for me, this scenario would repeat itself dozens of times over the course of the next few months. I believe that is how they acted on their agenda of making me ill both times. That negative energy of standing there, that close to me for hours. Well it was enough to affect my health for a period of months. It almost succeeded in ending my life both times. "They Watch your Every Move" (#10 of our Top Ten List)

October 22, 2020 was our 32nd wedding anniversary. My husband surprised me. He walked through my sister's door on Friday, the 23rd for a wonderful weekend together. On Saturday, October 24th, my sister was in her dressing room when our dead mother screamed her name hysterically five times in a row, "Pam! Pam! Pam! Pam! Pam!" Pam yelled, "Mom, what is it, what is it?" She heard nothing. We could not figure it out. It wasn't until much later we found out why Mom was so upset.

At the beginning of December 2020, my teeth implants needed to heal so I had a break before the next phase. Maybe my dentist just felt sorry for me because of my longing for my family. I drove home on December 12th with absolutely zero teeth in my mouth! I didn't care, (we had to wear face masks anyway, right?) I was so happy to be home, and for a full four weeks over the Christmas holiday! This was the first time I had been home since Sidekick had left.

I arrived home in the middle of the day, my daughter having just left for work. The house was empty. Actually, I was apprehensive. I tentatively walked into the back door. I stood there, moving my head from left to right and back again while taking deep breaths. Then a smile lit up my face. What a difference in energy! By the end of that evening, I knew the demons were still there, on the edges of my reality, but I could accept that scenario. No shoulder checking, no in-my-face intimidation and no touchy feely evil! Most of all, the Smoking Demon and his pet had vanished!

January 3, 2021, a week before I left Las Vegas to return to my sister's house to continue my dental work, I was sitting on the couch in the living room, just thinking, my thoughts centering on the past week of celebrations. I realized that after 23 precarious long months, for the first time in that house, I felt happiness! This was such an amazing achievement that immediately after I felt happiness, I felt shock.

All of this difference in energy would be short lived. Things were about to go south.

Sidekick was still coming in the house. One night around 2:00 am, I woke up in a panic, not understanding why. I came out to the living room, sat down on the couch, and tried to relax and bring the adrenaline down. I gazed up and saw a flash of movement at the top of the stairwell. I felt him before I saw him. I looked up and there was Sidekick at the top of the stairs. He stared down at me with such an intent gaze that I almost looked away. Then he dissipated! Gone! Despicable person that he was, how was he getting into the house? It looked like he had visited my daughter's bedroom. Strangely enough, a few days earlier, she told me she had felt him in her room during the middle of the night. Now I was not the only one seeing or feeling him!

I had been home three days when my sister phoned one morning. She was speaking excitedly concerning the window at the bottom of the stairs. "Check the locks on the windows!" she said. Apparently, my dead mother (I should just refer to her as DM, everything is an acronym these days) had told her that morning. Apparently, there was a window unlocked and Sidekick was physically coming in and out of it freely. My stomach just dropped as I slowly walked towards the window in question. Instead of checking the locks, I attempted to open it. It opened easily. It was not locked. Thank you, DM!

When I mentioned the unlocked window to my hubby and daughter, they looked so confused. They hadn't opened it in a while, they said. "Did anybody check to see if windows were locked after Sidekick left?" I asked. They did not. After everything I had told them, after everything he had done, they were still clueless!

When I called my sister to fill her in, she had another astonishing surprise for me. On October 24, 2020, when my dead mother shouted Pam's name five successive times, it was at that exact moment that Sidekick had opened that precise window and breached our home! OMG, my hair is standing up on my forearms just writing about it. This was so incredibly creepy! Did my daughter just feel him in her bedroom or was he really physically there? DM has not yet given me the much-needed answer to that question.

I will end this chapter with another very spine-chilling reality. A week after I returned home on December 12, 2020, I was dressing up for a nice holiday dinner. I opened up my jewelry chest to choose a necklace. Hanging there in a ritualistic fashion was my Mom's pearl necklace that Sidekick had stolen a year before!! I fell to my knees, a dozen thoughts racing through my head all at once! Silently, I cried. When will this bad dream, this nightmare end? My sister, however, being the more practical one, told me to get real. We did get Mom's pearls back!

1ˢᵗ John 4:4 "You, dear children, are from God and have overcome them, because the one who is in you is greater than the one who is in the world."

May 8th, 2021 at 11:00 am.

It is a beautiful Saturday morning. Pam and I are in a conference room located in Oakland, California with our hands clasped together praying consecutively along with other Christians in different locations.

This is a big deal!

After two years jam-packed with difficult times, God is dealing with my husband, the Demonic Fog and all other thingamajigs that are in him. At long last, my husband is upstairs with the Spiritual Healer being cleansed! An elongated, heartbreaking journey wrapped around a 32-year-old marriage, my husband's soul, and the much-craved revenge of a mentally ill Satan worshiper who believed if he couldn't have my daughter, then I didn't deserve my husband/marriage either, or my life.

We can just hear the muffled sound of voices coming from the office above, but nothing we can clearly comprehend. Hours and hours of deep prayer, crying and my personal agony have gone into this cleansing. We are completely confident in our faith that God will make my husband the man I knew when I married him. The promise God made to me when I left for my sister's house on September 20, 2020 meant the entire kit and caboodle at this moment. I was holding on tight to it. Get away from Hell's sublet so that I could properly take care of myself and he would deal with my husband and our marriage. My husband's soul being cleared was all part of that promise.

My husband and I had driven over 600 miles to have a person both my sister and I trusted to perform this awesome cleansing.

Again, this was a big deal!

However, I have told you, the reader, again and again that my husband felt there was absolutely nothing wrong with him. No depression, oppression or possession at all! And yet, he was a completely different person from who he was two years ago when he walked into this house. As previously discussed throughout this book, I knew that, at the very minimum, he was in a severe Demonic Fog.

Yes! A big deal indeed!

Ninety anxious minutes had elapsed when my husband opened the door to the conference room and walked in with a huge smile on his face! Involuntarily, I sucked my breathe in at the peace surrounding him. The positive energy flowing from his body was almost solid, it was so formidable. Thank you, God, for keeping your promise; at long last, I had my husband back.

Miracles are all around us. The first miracle was my husband agreeing to the cleansing. The second miracle was it working! I would find out later what a miracle it was indeed!

Dead silence in the car as we made our way back to the house.

I patiently waited for him to speak; to want to share his experience with me. Finally, he asked me why I wasn't questioning him about his cleansing. My reply was, "When you're ready, you can tell me."

What happened next was very surprising.

First, he told me that the Spiritual Healer had expressed that he was a negative on the demonic attachments. "No way!" I thought to myself. I had seen them all over his body trapped like demonic pieces of Velcro! Secondly, tears began to roll down his cheeks.

My husband is logic; I am passion. Personally, in the last two years nothing about the way he had behaved had been, at all, logical to me. As I began to cry with him, he approached the subject of the closeness of my death the previous holiday season. His exact words were, "What was I thinking? I almost let you die." I was ignorant in the way of explaining to him that his personal control had not been his, but Sidekick's.

When I did at last speak to the Healer, even after all Sidekick had done to me and every part of the crap I had seen and experienced, I was, in my soul, shocked at what she told me! As to not give Sidekick too much credit, I won't go into the serious detail concerning the power he possessed over my husband. After all, I have already expressed the power he held over me on numerous occasions.

My friend, the Spiritual Healer, has been doing cleansings for decades, learning her healing craft all over the world. When she told me that my husband had mojo in him that she had only heard about but had never actually encountered in person, I was speechless. Oh, and so many demons attached to him that he had to be cleared six times! My husband actually had demonic implants! Sidekick had been performing rituals on him for two solid years! The Healer had no choice but to tell him he had no attachments because she felt if she told him the truth, he would get up, run out and never come back. She focused on the weighty job ahead of her and nothing else. I thank God for her every day.

In my heart, I knew that both my husband and daughter necessitated a free two-year pass from God and myself for the Demonic Fog that Sidekick had surrounded them in, plus the sorcery. God had healed me in so many ways that I happily gave it to them both with love.

At last my husband was thinking again like the man I married.

The Demon blocks we experienced during the writing of this conclusion were unprecedented in their numbers!

One day, I was writing when chills and goose-bumps covered my body. Then an angelic voice said, "Do not be afraid. You are reacting to God's protections. You are safe." God's love is an amazing journey.

We feel a strong conviction here to actually share the story between God and Satan. Over the past two years, we have discovered their relationship is way more complicated than we first believed. Afterall, it began with God loving Lucifer very much. Lucifer's name in Heaven means "star of the morning."

After his fall from God's grace, he became known as Satan, which means "adversary." Lucifer had great beauty, power, wisdom and influence with God. He surrounded God's throne. However, Lucifer became so caught up in his power, beauty, intelligence, and the power that God had given him that it corrupted him with pride. He started to seek the glory and honor that God had for himself. We think that we have all experienced this type of person in our lives. Let's face it: Satan is the original narcissist!

We believe with all our hearts that God did not create Satan, Lucifer created Satan. I mean own it!

Now referred to as Satan (biggest liar/loser in the universe!), he now decides he wants/needs to be worshipped above God. Really? What idiot gives up a place right next to God?

Satan's power became so perverted and corrupt that God banished him from living in Heaven. Upon his departure, he took 1/3 of Heaven's angels with him, which turned into the demons that haunted us daily for 19 months! I will reiterate again, Satan's power is that of a fallen angel, not a God. There is one God and one God only in this universe.

Sidebar: Of all of the demons we have seen in the two separate households, not one of them had majestic wings like Archangel Michael in Chapter 4 "The Mighty Roar." Interesting.

The Bible says that Satan hates mankind because they worship God and not him. Satan wants to be the one mankind adores! Talk about an ego! He entices all types of people to serve him, weak or strong. He is ALL about the divide and conquer strategy. He tries his hardest to hurt God by division and hatred. The proof is in this book!

Bottom Line: Even though Satan's outcome is clearly defined in Revelations, his earthly agenda consists of complete destruction before God destroys him, his fallen angels and his precious SW's!

The Satan worshiper (SW) i.e., Sidekick, is not going to be high up in Hell as he repeatedly screamed at me! Consider the source of his wisdom! It's one of Satan's biggest lies! SW's will be thrown down into the lost sea of souls along with the rest of the losers who believe his lies and deceit! Accountability to God belongs to all of us, including fallen angels.

We begin by asking ourselves the life changing question: what is salvation? The Bible clearly says it's being saved from the consequences of our sin. However, for me, it's so much more than that. It's the beginning of a deep, complex connection with our Lord, but our sin prevents a relationship with him. The good news is that God sent his only precious Son to die for our sins so that we could have everlasting life, love and peace! Salvation is available to anyone including Satan worshipers! God does provide a way out of the spiritual self-destruction you are currently living in. His love and forgiveness are there for the asking. It's as simple as sincerely inviting him to fill your heart and life. God doesn't require you to sign a contract or to give in order to receive. After the horror of this book, our prayer is that each and every one of you will accept God's invitation. To God be the Glory!

GOD IS IN IT TO WIN IT!

SCRIPTURES TO CORROBORATE THE ABOVE STATEMENTS:

"Your heart became proud on account of your beauty, and you corrupted your wisdom because of your splendor."—
— *Ezekiel 28:17*

"And there was war in heaven: Michael and his angels fought against the dragon; and the dragon fought and his angels and prevailed not; neither was their place found any more in heaven. And the great dragon was cast out, that old serpent, called the Devil, and Satan, which deceiveth the whole world: he was cast out in the earth, and his angels were cast out with him."
— *Revelation 12:7-9*

"And he said unto them, I beheld Satan as lightening fall from heaven"
— *Luke 10:18*

"How art thou fallen from heaven, O Lucifer, son of the morning! How art thou cut down to the ground, which didst weaken the nations! For thou hast said in thine heart, I will ascend into heaven, I will exalt

my throne above the stars of God: I will sit also upon the mount of the congregation, in the sides of the north: I will ascend above the heights of the clouds; I will be like the most High."
— Isaiah 14:12-14

"Ye are of your father the devil, and the lusts of your father ye will do. He was a murderer from the beginning, and abode not in the truth, there is no truth in him. When he speaketh a lie, he speaketh of his own: for he is a liar, and the father of it"
— John 8:44

"Then shall he say also unto them on the left hand, Depart from me, Ye cursed, into everlasting fire, prepared for the devil and his angels."
— Matthew 25:41

"Seek ye the Lord while he may be found, call ye upon him while he is near: Let the wicked forsake his way, and the unrighteous man his thoughts: and let him return unto the Lord, and he will have mercy upon him; and to our God, for he will abundantly pardon."
— Isaiah 55:6-7

"For God so loved the world, that he gave his only begotten Son, that whosoever believeth in him should not perish, but have everlasting life."
— John 3:16

Below is our Top Ten List that we have accumulated based on our personal experiences over the past two years living with a Satan worshiper (SW). Here's our take on their dirty little secrets! Reading this book, look at how just one SW affected the lives of our family throughout the years. Just one! This list is a demonstration of spiritual warfare. We included Bible verses that will aid you in defeating a SW.

Let's go over our Top Ten List:

1. **Demonic Fog:** This places its victims in a false reality. The fog corresponds with their agenda. It could be an ER doctor or your husband of 32 years. No one comprehends what is really happening to or around them, i.e., the Demonic Fog. Out of the entire Top Ten List, this was the most devastating to us, especially concerning my husband. It leaves you alone, thinking you are crazy with no one believing you. It had the most damaging effect on all of our lives. Chapter 8 is a great example of a Demonic Fog.

2. **Physically and Mentally Intimidate:** This can be accomplished by a strong evil presence that makes you sick to your stomach. This is where the eight-foot shadow man, hellhound, or maybe even a ZoZo come into play. Sometimes the evil comes right up behind you which we call "Shoulder Checking." The fear you feel from this can be so paralyzing. Both my sister and I believe that in Chapter 10 and Chapter 11 we were actually dealing with the Big Kahuna, Satan itself. I actually believe I saw it (See Illustration) and Pam felt it at Big Bear.

3. **Revenge/Retaliation:** I believe "Our Light Bulb Moment" (Chapter 10) demonstrates their need for this perfectly. Sidekick planned this particular revenge for years. Again, devastating to my husband and me.

4. **Disastrous Agendas for Victims:** So much effort was

placed into Sidekick trying to kill me. Whenever I would reach out for help, whoever it was would be viciously attacked. Due to privacy we didn't include some stories in the book. The one that really blew my mind though, was the demonologist.

5. **Device/Electronics Manipulators** (even Medical Devices): Manipulating electronics even Medical Devices. They tried to kill my sister twice by manipulating her insulin pump (Chapter 8), programing it to shoot extra units of insulin into her. Two weeks ago, I went on an insulin pump and I can tell you it is not as easy as pushing a button or two. There are a number of steps you have to scroll through. At the end of the process the pumps actually asks you if you want to deliver the insulin. This was such a WOW moment for both of us.

6. **Transforms into Different Images:** A demon taking on the look of another person is completely frightening. Twice my sister thought she was looking at me. Once from her security camera when she saw me in the backyard smoking when I was not. The second time walking through her bedroom in the middle of the night. We have found that the purpose of these transformations is usually to cause trouble. Other times, demons have taken the form of a dead friend and even our dead mother.

7. **Send Their Pets to Terrorize You:** This one makes me laugh at the same time it terrorizes me! We have seen Hellhounds, grasshoppers with demon heads on them, two-foot diameter spikey spiders, and miniature dinosaurs with wings, Dino.

8. **Play Mind Games:** There is the biblical question if Satan can or cannot read our thoughts, but he has scrutinized human behavior for thousands of years. For him, we are not that complicated. Your vulnerability will become his power if you allow it. A solid example of what I am speaking of was all the conflict between my sister and me. They went way out of their way to break us apart so I would have no support at all. Demons are very capable of influencing your thinking in dark, negative, incomprehensible ways.

9. **Energy Drainers:** Nineteen months of energy drainers and plus some! #9 consumes our entire book! It consumed me! First, they would drain my energy, not allowing me to sleep or rest. They would stand in the corner of my bedroom or even get in bed with me to watch and drain me. That is when they started with the #8 on the list, Mind Games.

10. **They Watch your Every Move:** Oh, how I wish this was just paranoia, but unfortunately it is not. This sounds so crazy, but I feel that the demons reported back to him incessantly whenever he needed them to, just like Harry Potter's owl. Just two weeks ago, my sister and her husband were visiting us in Las Vegas. We were all sitting in the living room laughing and talking when my sister looked up at the stairs and there was the same demon I see almost every night standing halfway down the stairs bent over the railing watching and listening to us like a Roman centurion.

HOW TO PROTECT YOURSELVES FROM THE TOP TEN LIST:

- The best way to protect yourself from our Top Ten List is to call on God. Everyday take the time to pray and ask God to send all spiritual helpers, angels, and other guides to shield and surround you from the evil.
- Read God's word—it is powerful.
- Play Christian music in your home and vehicle.
- Show no fear when evil comes into your life. Fear empowers them, makes them stronger. God gives you the power over evil.

> *(Ephesians 6:11-18* "11 Put on the full armor of God, so that you can take your stand against the devil's schemes. 12 For our struggle is not against flesh and blood, but against the rulers, against the authorities, against the powers of this dark world and against the spiritual forces of evil in the heavenly realms. 13 Therefore put on the full armor of God, so that when the day of evil comes, you may be able to stand your ground, and after you have done everything, to stand. 14 Stand firm then, with the belt of truth buckled around your waist, with the breastplate of righteousness in place, 15 and with your feet fitted with the readiness that comes from the gospel of peace. 16 In addition to all this, take up the shield of faith, with which you can

extinguish all the flaming arrows of the evil one. [17] Take the helmet of salvation and the *sword of the Spirit, which is the word of God.* [18] And pray in the Spirit on all occasions with all kinds of prayers and requests. With this in mind, be alert and always keep on praying for all the Lord's people.")

EPILOGUE

My daughter never felt the same about her beautiful home again. Because of lingering energies that some used homes can possess, it was essential to my daughter to buy a brand-new house clear of any mischief. This makes what Sidekick did all the worse.

She repaired the damage that Sidekick had created during his meltdowns. Had the house blessed, put it on the market, and sold it within days.

During the moving process, ritualistic items were found hidden in various places. Pictured below is one of them; a paper satchel that was stuffed in the back of my daughter's desk. When we opened it up there were pieces of a special candy that she had bought Sidekick, her hair tie with hair in it (DNA) and broken glass. This was all wrapped up in papyrus paper, ball shaped. My daughter placed it outside the front door in a pot until she could properly get rid of it however the next morning both the pot and satchel had disappeared.

As a Christian she moved on with her life.

My sister and I were overwhelmingly terrified after Sidekick repeatedly had bragged to me about killing thirteen people. We filed two reports with the FBI on this matter. He vowed to seek revenge.

I do not know how, but he quickly learned our new whereabouts after we moved. Unfortunately, Satan and Sidekick are up to their old tricks again however he has lost much of his power by not having been (and never will be) in the new home.

My sister and I have so many questions that only God can answer. Maybe in time he will bless us with total closure on this chapter of our lives.

After reading our book if you feel you have some answers for us, please go to our website: www.thehauntingsoftwosisters.com and share your story. We would love to hear from you.

Pam and Karen 2020

*Strange rock found up against new house by
front door during our first week there.*

Made in the USA
Columbia, SC
22 July 2021

42229441R00141